Teachers as Leaders

Teachers as Leaders:
Evolving Roles

E D I T O R

Carol Livingston

Robert M. McClure
NEA Mastery In Learning Consortium
NEA National Center for Innovation
Series Editor

nea PROFESSIONAL LIBRARY
National Education Association
Washington, D.C.

Printing History
    First Printing: April 1992

Note

The opinions expressed in this publication should not be construed as representing the policy or position of the National Education Association. Materials published by the NEA Professional Library are intended to be discussion documents for educators who are concerned with specialized interests of the profession.

Library of Congress Cataloging-in-Publication Data

Teachers as leaders: evolving roles / editor, Carol Livingston.
        p. cm. — (NEA school restructuring series)
        Includes bibliographical references.
        ISBN 0-8106-1848-6
        1.   Teachers — United States.   2. Leadership.
I. Livingston, Carol.   II. Series.
LB1775.2.T46   1992
371.1'04'0973—dc20

91-28909
CIP

CONTENTS

FOREWORD

The intense interest in restructuring and improving our schools is fueled by many teacher leaders throughout the country, several of whom have authored this book. In each of the cases here, there is a glimpse of what schools will become when faculties have opportunities to develop and nurture leadership from within themselves. One of these teachers, Eliot Wigginton, writes about a faculty as ". . . a collection of fairly remarkable people who represent strengths and solutions to all our problems."

There are many reasons why stronger teacher leadership is needed inside of schools. One of these is that we simply must do better at keeping energetic, resourceful, caring people with students. Business as usual—with teachers being isolated from one another, with rewards reserved for those at too far a distance from students, with teachers being separated from opportunities for self-development—will not keep good people in the classroom. Despite the frustrations of becoming a teacher leader—often in a hostile environment, as seen in the cases here—these stories point the way toward schools enjoying the benefits of these new roles.

Perhaps an even more compelling reason to seek greater opportunities for teachers to become leaders is the impact on teaching and learning. The old cliché, "we behave as we are treated" applies to teachers and their teaching as surely as to anyone. We know that in schools where the principal shares leadership with the faculty that teachers are more likely to be democratic in their dealings with students (and with parents, too). It seems likely that such behaviors are contagious, that older students will be less "bossy" with younger ones in such an environment. Democratic cultures are more empowering for all within them than are authoritarian ones.

There are wonderful stories in this book, and they are all true. Now, we know that schools are better when they are inhabited by strong teacher leaders. What remains for those schools that do not now have such leadership is, as the footwear commercial admonishes, DO IT.

—Robert McClure
Series Editor

INTRODUCTION: TEACHER LEADERSHIP FOR RESTRUCTURED SCHOOLS

Teachers are experts with special talents and a deep commitment for educating new generations. That commitment is best accomplished in a professional, collaborative environment in which teacher leadership sparks enthusiasm for teaching, and in turn, motivates students to realize their fullest potential. (From the Teacher Leadership Philosophy Statement of the Medina Project, Puget Sound Educational Consortium; Diercks and colleagues 1988)

Teacher leadership is not a novel idea. Teachers have long served as association leaders, team leaders, department chairs, curriculum developers and, more recently, as designers of staff development. Yet, one might legitimately ask, "Leadership by whose warrant and to what end?"

Beyond the walls of the classroom, teacher leadership roles have been limited in scope. With the exception of union or association leadership, most teacher leadership roles have existed at administrative prerogative within a hierarchical structure of decision making. Most have involved minimal levels of collegial or collaborative involvement and little or no training. Many team leader and department chair roles are predominantly clerical or managerial in function.

Although it has been recognized for decades that teacher participation in curriculum development is vital, too often that participation has been limited to token involvement toward implementation of a centrally-determined curriculum. Teachers are often *representatives* (sometimes reluctant) of a staff or department rather than *leaders* who collaborate with their peers

9

in the development of curriculum. Finally, most extended teacher leadership roles are continuous as opposed to rotating or flexible; and, for many teachers, the "step up" to leadership has required the "step out" of the classroom.

EXPANDING OPPORTUNITIES FOR TEACHER LEADERSHIP

Recently, there have been calls for expanded and qualitatively different leadership opportunities for teachers. With the realization that legislated reforms address—at best—minimum standards, the nation is coming to realize a need for more authentic forms of school reform or restructuring to meet the needs of an increasingly diverse student population and our rapidly changing society.

Proponents of the second wave of school reform and recent reports on the reform of teacher education call for dramatically different approaches to educational change. In particular, they focus on increasing the professionalism of teaching and teachers, encouraging and supporting the ongoing learning and development of teachers, and developing new leadership opportunities and roles for them (e.g., Carnegie 1986; Darling-Hammond 1987; Elmore and McLaughlin 1988; Lieberman 1988; Holmes Group 1986).

These recommendations for teacher professionalism and leadership reflect the understanding that curriculum and instruction should be responsive to the learners and to the particular school and community context; and thus, decisions about curriculum and instruction should be made by those closest to the learners. The call is motivated, as well, by a recognition that the profession of teaching cannot attract and keep talented teachers if the role is paraprofessional. Teachers should not have to abandon the classroom to engage in school-wide decision making and to exercise leadership roles. Now, more than ever, the nation needs excellent teachers.

Some, who may fear the emasculation of administrative leadership, maintain the call for shared decision making and increased teacher leadership is the latest dangerous fad in school improvement (see, for example, Geisert 1980). Ironically, the very body of research that led to the "Principal as Instructional Leader" movement, may provide support to extend leadership roles to teachers. Reanalysis of the school effectiveness data demonstrates that shared governance characterized many of the effective schools. The essential conclusion, then, is that effective schools require strong instructional leadership—not necessarily that the principal must be the instructional leader (Stedman 1987). Further support for shared leadership is derived from modern management theory which recognizes that shared power strengthens an organization (e.g. Ouchi 1981).

The variety of opportunities for teacher leadership has increased in recent years. Teachers are becoming involved in educational decision making and school improvement. Teachers have become research colleagues, advisors and mentors, master teachers, members of school-based leadership teams and instructional support teams, and change facilitators.

Yet teacher leadership remains a *hot* topic. The possibilities and benefits of new leadership roles for teachers intertwine with the constraints and tensions of existing tasks, responsibilities, and relationships. The reasons for these constraints and tensions become apparent when we examine our metaphors for schooling and the teacher roles circumscribed by these ways of thinking.

TEACHER LEADERSHIP IN THE METAPHORS FOR SCHOOLING

Metaphor is a powerful, often unconscious, tool in human thought and communication. Metaphors structure our thinking, focus our interpretation of events and experiences, and consequently guide our behavior (Lakoff and Johnson 1980). Essential, therefore, to revisioning and restructuring our schools, is the examination of the metaphors we use to think about schooling.

Schools as Factories

The factory (machine) metaphor has dominated the American educational scene for over half a century. In this image, education is a bureaucratic and highly rationalized enterprise. Outcomes are standardized and defined in terms of productivity, effectiveness, and efficiency. Quality control is achieved through tight supervision and application of scientific management principles. Personnel functions are standardized and characterized by differentiation and specialization. Decision making is linear and hierarchical. Teachers are compliant production-line laborers, and students are the products—compliant receivers—of the educational production process.

In the factory metaphor, teachers (labor) are a cost rather than a resource. Teacher leaders, in effect, become line supervisors. By rising in the hierarchy, they are removed from direct production (teaching) and lose the credibility of "oneness" with their peers.

The machine metaphor does not account adequately for the complexity of schools as they exist, and certainly not for what we wish them to be. Yet, most of the legislated reforms of the 1980's are consistent with the metaphor. Some of the recommendations for teacher leadership positions (lead teachers and career ladders, for example) reflect its hierarchical orientation. Furthermore, research has documented the pervasive influence of the factory metaphor in educational research, policy, administrative and classroom practice, and instructional discourse (see for example, the Spring 1990 issue of *Theory Into Practice*).

Only if we change our dominant metaphor are we likely to encourage the self-development of autonomous learners who possess the knowledge and skills to participate in a technologically sophisticated, socially complex democratic society. Changing metaphors is a complex and difficult task but, clearly, a necessary one.

Schools as Complex Organisms

Discussions of reform in education draw generally upon one of two metaphors for schools: school as factory or school as organism (Schwarz 1991). In the organic metaphor, schools are seen as complex systems composed of interdependent parts, changing and evolving together in response to demands coming both from within the system and from outside it. Decisions are generally made by those who implement them, and authority relationships need not be hierarchical. In this vision, teachers are autonomous professionals, free to design curriculum and instruction in response to the unique needs and interests of their students and the social context.

Clearly, the traditional culture of professional educators identifies more greatly with this metaphor, as do the calls for second-wave reform. The metaphor captures the responsiveness and flexibility of desired educational processes, but what of the nature of education itself? What are the bounds of autonomy? How do the various parts interrelate and function together? Can the organization of schools be this flat? What is the role of teacher leadership or any leadership, for that matter?

Schools as Knowledge Work Organizations

Educational reformer, Philip Schlechty (1984) claims that the dichotomy between centralization and decentralization is a false one. He proposes that our dominant (factory) metaphor be transformed to envision students as skilled knowledge workers, teachers as first-line supervisors or executives, and principals as managers of managers. In this conceptualization, students are more productive because they have greater control over the conditions of work and the types of products produced.

The student-as-knowledge-worker metaphor attends more specifically to the central task of schools. It respects

13

students as thinkers and teachers as responsible professionals. This conceptualization remains, however, fundamentally hierarchical and linked to images of the corporate world. The role of teacher leader is unclear.

Schools as Learning Places

Perhaps, we should move away from organizational and production metaphors toward ones that are more functional. Drawing upon classroom studies and research on learning from cognitive and social constructivist perspectives, Hermine Marshall (1990) advocates that we reconceptualize schools as *learning places* rather than *work places*. In schools as learning places, as in the organic metaphor, authority relationships are less hierarchical, more responsive, and more functional—authoritative rather then authoritarian—in the classroom and across the school. However, in this conceptualization, schools are *centers of inquiry* for adults and students. The school-as-learning-place metaphor honors the central task of schooling and models life-long learning. It opens the possibilities for new forms of leadership and provides a powerful way to consider the relationship between teacher leadership and student learning.

No single metaphor seems adequate to describe schools and educational systems in this country as they are; nor have educators or their stakeholders agreed upon a single guiding vision. Teacher leadership will both shape and be shaped by the metaphors that drive educational thinking and practice.

THE CONTRIBUTION AND ORGANIZATION OF THIS BOOK

This volume explores the phenomenon of teacher leadership in schools that are changing, improving, and restructuring—that is, of teacher leaders negotiating new metaphors. The chapters help us understand the nature, problems, and possibilities of teacher leadership and enhance our understanding of educational change at its core.

Part One provides an in-depth examination of teacher leadership as it exists in practice and in the dreams of teachers who are leading change. The five chapters are based upon a series of case studies conceived and conducted independently, each with a slightly different question or focus, but all derived from a commitment to understand the nature and contribution of teacher leadership in school change.

Methodologically, the chapters represent different approaches to case study research. The cases were constructed from data drawn from a wide variety of geographic and demographic sites in the United States and Canada. The data collection and analysis methods used in the construction of the cases range from traditional interview methods and reliance on the tools of participant observation to newer methods utilizing autobiographical narrative. The chapters share a style which is intentionally descriptive—"thick" by standards of economy and efficiency—and enriched with passages in teacher leaders' own words. That, the authors know, is the only way to represent with authenticity the highly complex, contextual, connected, and evolving world of teacher leadership.

In Part Two, two advocates for teacher collaboration and leadership in learner-centered schools reflect on the previous chapters. Representing the perspectives of theory and practice, the authors consider what we have learned about teacher leadership and envision its future.

Although each chapter in this volume can stand alone, the reader is encouraged to read the volume in its entirety. The power of this collection lies in the commonality of themes and issues across the separate chapters:

- leadership, collaboration and colleagueship;

- leadership as inside or outside, formal or emergent, hierarchical or non-hierarchical;

- requirements for knowledge and skill;

- workplace culture as both prerequisite and outcome;

- issues of legitimacy and authority, empowerment and voice, role negotiation, and time;

- personal impact of leadership;

- the relationship between the missions of teaching and leading; and, ultimately,

- the impact of teacher leadership on student learning.

Teachers as Leaders: Evolving Roles will be of interest to a wide variety of audiences: It will inform education policy makers who are at the forefront in promoting a vision—a new metaphor—for the way we think about and conduct the education enterprise and who are, in a pragmatic vein, concerned with attracting and retaining "the best and the brightest." Teacher educators will find insights into essential skills and knowledge for teacher leadership. For those in decision-making and administrative positions in school systems and associations, the volume will affirm the power of authentic teacher leadership; it will assist them in envisioning the forms that teacher leadership might take and the structures which may support or inhibit it. The accounts will provide hope and inspiration to a large number of classroom teachers who have no desire to leave the classroom, yet long for greater connectedness with their colleagues and with educational issues, at large. The chapters will resonate with the experiences of classroom teachers who are balancing the demands of instruction and leadership and pose alternatives for reflection. Finally, it will strike a chord with a large group of veteran *former* teachers who, like myself, relinquished parts of their souls when they left the classroom to pursue leadership roles and who advocate expanded opportunities for teachers as leaders.

—Carol Livingston
Editor

REFERENCES

Carnegie Foundation for the Advancement of Teaching. 1986. *A nation prepared: Teachers for the twenty-first century.* New York: The Foundation.

Darling-Hammond, L. 1987. Schools for tomorrow's teachers. *Teachers College Record* 88: 354–358.

Diercks, K.; Dillard, S.; McElliott, K.; Morgan, J.; Schulz, B.; Tipps, L.; and Wallentine, K. 1988. *Teacher leadership: Commitment and challenge.* Seattle: Puget Sound Educational Consortium.

Elmore, R. F., and McLaughlin, M. 1988. *Steady work: Policy, practice, and the reform of American education.* Santa Monica, Calif.: Rand.

Geisert, G. 1980. Participatory management: Panacea or hoax? *Educational Leadership* 38(3): 56–59.

Holmes Group. 1986. *Tomorrow's teachers: A report of the Holmes Group.* East Lansing, Mich.: The Group.

Lakoff, G., and Johnson, M. 1980. *Metaphors we live by.* Chicago: University of Chicago Press.

Lieberman, A., ed. 1988. *Building a professional culture in schools.* New York: Teachers College Press.

Marshall, H. H. 1990. Beyond the workplace metaphor: The classroom as a learning setting. *Theory Into Practice* 29:94–101.

Ouichi, W. 1981. *Theory Z.* Reading, Mass.: Addison-Wesley.

Schlechty, P. C. 1984. Images of schools. *Teachers College Record* 86: 156–170.

Schwarz, A. J. 1991. Organizational metaphors, curriculum reform, and local school and district changes. In *The politics of curriculum decision making: Issues in centralizing the curriculum,* ed. M. F. Klein, 167–197. Albany, N.Y.: State University of New York Press.

Stedman, L. C. 1987. It's time we changed the effective schools formula. *Phi Delta Kappan* 69: 215–224.

Part One:
TEACHERS AS LEADERS

Chapter 1

WORKING TOGETHER: TEACHER LEADERSHIP AND COLLABORATION

by Patricia A. Wasley

Teacher leadership is defined as influencing and engaging colleagues toward improved practice. Ted, Gwen, and Mary each held different kinds of leadership roles and worked in collaborative relationships with their colleagues in order to enhance learning experiences for students. Analysis of their roles and experiences suggests four principles for developing more powerful leadership roles for teachers: (1) Many teachers do not want to leave the classroom or undertake management functions to exercise leadership. (2) Teacher leaders must have legitimate power, derived from their peers. (3) Teachers are interested in learning opportunities that allow them to collaborate with their peers. (4) Different collaborative relationships (e.g., mentoring, division of labor, and partnering) offer different incentives and leadership opportunities.

When I was teaching at the high school level not so very long ago, my colleagues and I worked almost exclusively in our own classrooms with our students. We worked in a hierarchical system where the principal was the "leader" whether we liked him or not. We saw department head positions as the only leadership opportunities available for teachers (although, because department heads tended to hold onto their positions for life, even those opportunities were infrequent). The work of department heads was primarily administrative—they ordered books, lobbied for resources, called the department meetings where we determined who would use what books when. If someone had asked me then what kinds of leadership roles teachers should fill, I would have said that teachers ought to be leading their kids towards better learning.

Recently, the discussion about teacher leadership has taken a new turn. Teachers, many are now saying, should be leading their colleagues towards building more powerful schools. The national call for leadership positions for teachers (see Carnegie Foundation 1986; Holmes Group 1986) suggests "career ladder" opportunities—mentoring, expert/novice relationships, teachers implementing staff development programs. These suggestions raise a number of tough puzzles and confounding dilemmas.

One of the dilemmas stems from the fact that most of these kinds of positions already exist in schools. Teachers are currently mentoring their colleagues and conducting staff development activities. So what's the difference between the roles that exist and the new roles suggested?

The second puzzle is a real stickler. The suggestions for teacher leadership positions are hierarchical in nature—one teacher assists colleagues in their practice of cooperative learning, or through their first year of teaching, by applying for a position that is a "rung up the ladder" and, in some cases, out of the classroom. Teachers, on the other hand, have indicated that they are not greatly interested in hierarchical career ladders. Instead, they are interested in finding more powerful ways of facilitating learning for their students; and in doing so they would like more opportunities to collaborate with their colleagues, and—they'd like to stay in the classroom (see McLaughlin and Yee 1988; Bacharach 1986).

There are also several missing pieces to this teacher leadership puzzle. One is that it isn't at all clear what people mean by "collaboration." Second, it isn't at all clear what the relationship is between teacher leadership and collaboration. If teachers believe that the best way to improve schools is to collaborate with their colleagues, do they want teacher leadership positions and, if so, what might they look like?

In order to search for some potential puzzle pieces, I first looked for a working definition of leadership. A search through the literature on leadership revealed that leaders are commonly described as having the ability to engage their colleagues in change. Leaders influence people to do things they would not ordinarily do and leaders have a source of power that gives them the ability to influence their colleagues (see Bass 1981).

With that clarification, I developed the following set of questions to guide my study of teacher leadership:

1. What kind of work do teacher leaders do?

2. How do they collaborate with their colleagues?

3. How do their colleagues feel about these collaborative arrangements?

4. What is the relationship between collaboration and leadership?

5. What kinds of collaborative relationships provide the greatest opportunity to influence changes in practice?

6. How do answers to these questions relate to the national call for teacher leadership positions?

I then selected three teacher leaders for study who were currently practicing in public schools in various parts of the country. Each held a very different kind of leadership role, but all were working in collaborative relationships with their colleagues in the hopes of providing better instruction for kids. All three were considered to be leaders by both administrators and teachers. I spent two weeks with each teacher, observing and interviewing them and several of their colleagues. All have been given pseudonyms for the purposes of this paper. (For the complete report from this study, see Wasley 1991.)

So that the reader can track the discoveries I made, I would like first to share a little about each of the teacher leaders and the contexts in which they work. I have included a brief snapshot of a day in their classrooms, along with a summary of their colleagues' responses to their teacher leadership roles. This information provides answers to the first three questions posed above.

The remainder of the chapter looks for answers to the last three guiding questions by exploring the kinds of collaborative relationships I discovered, the sources of power each teacher leader had, and how each source is related to teacher leadership—to a teacher's ability to influence colleagues towards improved practice.

THREE TEACHER LEADERS

Ted Smith, Gwen Ingman, and Mary Jones were all veteran teachers who held very different leadership positions. The diversity of their positions was appealing because I believed it would help us to become familiar with a range of possibilities. Each was a member of the state affiliate of the National Education Association. Each was perceived to be a leader by both administrators and teachers within his or her own district. Each taught in the classroom half time and was on half-time release to fulfill his or her leadership responsibilities.

Ted Smith had been teaching for twenty-two years at the high school level in a rural southeastern community and had gained national recognition for his work with students. The success of his work with students had allowed him to form a sort of school-within-a-school and to create an outside educational corporation of which he was president. He taught four classes per day in the local high school; he held no formal leadership position within his school although he was the senior staff person. The rest of his time was spent running the corporation; in addition to hiring teachers for the local high school who taught according to his philosophy, his responsibilities included working with a board of directors, securing funding from outside sources, and overseeing a large budget that supported a variety of activities.

In an attempt to spread his very successful teaching philosophy, he taught college courses in a number of states. To sustain teachers after they had completed the course, he organized support staff who coordinated ongoing teacher networks for those teachers who wished to continue to experiment with his methodology.

Ted was selected for our study because his position was self-created and provided enormous leadership for teachers around the country, while he functioned as a regular teacher within his own system.

Gwen Ingman taught in a rural elementary school and was just finishing her tenth year. She had been appointed to one of several half-time specialist positions as Instructional Support Teacher (IST), in order to support other teachers in their practice of Madeline Hunter's approach to teaching, "Instructional Theory into Practice" (ITIP). The positions were formal, created by the central office at the ratio of one teacher specialist per building. A teaching librarian in the morning, Gwen visited other teachers' classrooms in the afternoon to observe and to suggest such techniques as teaching to objectives, anticipatory set, monitoring, adjusting, and reteaching. This position was designed to support better instruction and to provide teachers with more collegial opportunities. Once during each school year, Gwen taught a college course in ITIP that was required for teachers in the district.

The IST positions had been subject to some controversy when instituted three years earlier, but were officially reported to be very successful and well supported at the time of the study. Gwen's case was particularly interesting because there were rumors afloat that the position was still not supported by the teachers.

Mary Jones had been teaching middle school students for thirty years. The western suburban school district in which she taught was undergoing a shift from suburban affluence to urban complexity. Mary had originally applied and been hired for a position as a teacher on special assignment, a formal leadership position created in her district by central office administrators. In that position, her responsibility was to provide instructional support for teachers (IST) to help them to experiment with new methodologies. Each teacher with whom Mary worked could indicate areas of interest; her job was to supply information, resources, and modeling.

After four years, Mary did not believe that the position was working well. Other teachers were not taking advantage of the IST's expertise or, when they did invite Mary into their classrooms to work, they often used it as catch-up time rather than as professional development time. As a result, she and a fellow specialist designed an experimental project where they would team-teach 60 heterogeneously mixed students, using a variety of instructional techniques and an integrated approach to the curriculum. The classroom was to be a demonstration center for other teachers—a place where they could come to observe and to experiment themselves. Mary also did in-service presentations for other teachers within her district and taught a variety of courses in her own and neighboring districts. Her case was particularly interesting because she had exercised some leadership in redesigning her leadership position.

SNAPSHOTS OF THREE TEACHER LEADERS

Ted Smith: An Entrepreneurial Teacher Leader

Ted Smith arrived at his office at 8:00 a.m. The office was a reconstructed log cabin set in the midst of 150 acres on a hillside in a rural, southern Appalachian community. The land had been purchased by Ted's corporation, Talking Mountain, to house their offices and to serve as a kind of museum for the collections of mountain artifacts he and his students collected over the years. The office building sat in among 26 other

26

reconstructed log cabins, spread out but visible in the distance. It was silent there, calm, except for the chittering birds. A lazy cat rolled in a bed of catnip near the cabin door.

Each morning Ted met for an hour and a half with the Talking Mountain support staff to review budgets, set schedules, arrange travel, check on publication schedules, and check their own documentation of their work and progress. On this day, he and Kate, his office manager, scheduled four meetings for the following Wednesday when he would be in the nearby metropolitan area to teach a college course for teachers. The course walked teachers through the process of building curriculum and instruction using John Dewey's educational philosophy. The meetings would enable him to contact a major source of potential funding: two potential board members and a current board member who advised them on their trust accounts.

Ted paused for some light-hearted chat with the staff before racing off to the local high school some ten miles down the road. As he arrived, his second-period class was already at work, some spread out on the floor, some in a makeshift darkroom that protruded into the middle of the room, some at computers at the back of the room. Betty, another Talking Mountain teacher who team-taught with Ted, was busy with the students at the computers. Ted circled the room, checking on the progress of each of the groups. The room buzzed with conversation and quiet industry.

These students generated a magazine four times a year. They determined the focus, researched the articles, conducted interviews, transcribed the tapes, and then wrote and edited their final articles. In addition, they did their own layout and photography work. Ted worked with each group as they needed help, and in spare moments organized the stacks of papers, books, and lesson plans on his own desk. At the end of the period, these students left and another group came in.

This next group was a college preparatory research class. Ted helped the students generate questions and organize them into an interview for the impending visit of a local Cherokee

Indian. He facilitated the discussion for the students while sitting on the floor amongst the group. The atmosphere was relaxed, yet they accomplished a great deal. At the end of the lesson he asked them to describe the steps they had just been through in the generation of an interview: brainstorm interest areas, formulate questions, organize the questions into categories of related topics, refine the questions, and put them into sequence.

After a five-minute break, another large group of students piled into the class. This was a first-year Talking Mountain class which focused on magazine production. Two other Talking Mountain teachers joined Ted to team-teach this group. Ted waited for quiet and then had each group report where it was on its particular project. The class reviewed deadlines and who was to go where and then divided, some staying in Ted's room, some disappearing with each of the other two teachers. He reminded them that they needed to reconvene for the last ten minutes of class to visit with a group of eleven teachers who were to arrive momentarily from two neighboring states. Again, Ted ranged the group to help students.

At the end of the period, the group reconvened to visit with the teachers, who had taken Ted's course and belonged to one of the Outreach Networks. They asked the students a variety of questions about their work and whether they liked this particular way of learning. The students answered with confidence and enthusiasm, noting that they worked far more hours in this class than they did in others because they were interested in the material. When the bell rang, the class disappeared and Ted dispersed the visiting teachers to observe other Talking Mountain classes that were in session.

After a noisy half-hour break for lunch in the school cafeteria, Ted met his fourth class of the day, another college preparatory English class. This group was working on different kinds of essays. Ted demonstrated how the assignment might be approached and then went over the evaluation criteria. This was a negotiating process: he asked them to change anything they did not understand and to suggest options which they felt would be more appropriate.

Sixth period was Ted's planning period, which he shared with Frank and Tom, his co-teachers. They reviewed their progress with their third-period classes, focusing on which students needed what kind of help and which of the teachers was best suited to give it. They then reviewed their individual curriculum writing projects; each was writing a guide for teachers describing the teaching process they used in a variety of disciplines.

Ted was interrupted by a visitor. Then another teacher from a neighboring district came in to talk with Ted about how teachers might arrange more entrepreneurial settings. He was impressed by Ted's ability to create his own job and wished to try to bend traditional working structures in schools in a similar way. Ted shared his experiences, but felt a bit at a loss to answer such a large question. As that visitor left, another walked in—a teacher who was applying for a recently vacated department head position at the school. He wanted to talk with Ted about his programs and about the school at large, because Ted's classes fit into the regular curriculum at the school. As the bell rang marking the end of the day, a parent walked in with her son to help him type a manuscript into the computer. The special education teacher came down to visit; she had taken Ted's course and was doing a project with her students. They talked about her progress.

A few minutes later, the secretary came over the loudspeaker announcing a faculty meeting in the library. All the teachers groaned and headed down to the meeting, during which the principal warned everyone to keep the kids busy right up to the end of the school year and gave them a pop quiz on their familiarity with the state curriculum guidelines. Ted played no active part in the meeting.

After the faculty meeting, Ted and his colleagues reconvened in his classroom, where the entire Talking Mountain staff was assembling for their weekly meeting to review the various projects they had under way. As they wandered in, each member wrote agenda items on the board. One of the staff took responsibility for facilitating the meeting, a responsibility which rotated throughout the staff. They prioritized the agenda and then discussed their work until 7:00 p.m. Most of the discussion centered around students and finding the right kind of assistance for them. All decisions were reached by consensus.

Ted left promptly to meet with the visiting teachers who were staying at a guest house on the Talking Mountain property. The group included ten teachers and the Outreach Network coordinator. In an informal discussion, the teachers asked questions about the Talking Mountain classes at Ted's school. In turn, he asked them questions about their own projects. The conversation was still going strong when Ted slipped out the door at around 10:00 p.m. He still had a stack of papers to grade before school the next morning.

Ted's Colleagues

I interviewed four of Ted's school colleagues, whom he identified respectively as a supporter of his work, someone who was indifferent to his work, the building association representative, and someone who was not supportive. Interestingly enough, all perceived Ted as a leader. Perhaps because he did not have a formal leadership position in the school and because his work did not impact their classes in any way, they were most supportive of everything he did. All of them had taken his class. Only one of them said that her teaching had changed substantially because of it. One of the teachers indicated that she already taught that way, while the others found the class to be stimulating. Several of them noted that it was the best college class they had ever had. They perceived Ted to be a leader because he had the courage to do things differently, because he brought information to them from other schools all across the country, and because he exposed them to the hundreds of visiting educators who trooped through his classroom every year. They also saw him as a leader because he was able to accomplish so much with his students.

Gwen Ingman: A Teacher Leader in a Principal's Model

Gwen arrived in her office in the library at 8:00 a.m. Although classes would not start until 9:00, she had a number of things to do to keep the library running smoothly, to prepare for her teaching responsibilities, and to get ready for the additional responsibilities that were part of her leadership role. She glanced around the office, she checked her "to-do" list, and laminated a few books while talking to the library aide about what needed to be done. A parent came in to discuss plans for an upcoming event. Gwen continued laminating books while they visited.

Gwen shared responsibility for the library with Jane, a morning kindergarten teacher. So that the rest of the faculty could have a badly needed half-hour of planning time each week, she and Jane taught all the students in the school for one half-hour session a week in the library. Jane took the majority of the primary students; Gwen took the intermediate students. Each day, Gwen taught four or five classes in the morning; Jane took over in the afternoon. Gwen and Jane divided the work of running the library. Gwen had responsibility for the audio-visual equipment, for checking in new books, and for coordinating the library aides. Jane was in charge of ordering new materials, shelving procedures, and the library inventory.

Gwen's first class was a group of kindergartners. They tiptoed in and sang a song about being quiet in the library. She spent the first ten minutes checking in books they had taken out and reviewing their plans for the day. The next ten minutes were spent looking for new books. Gwen wandered among the students, reminding them to be quiet and helping them to find good selections. For the last ten minutes, Gwen read a story the children had illustrated the week before. They held up their pictures at the right moment in the story. They clearly thought this was fun. Class over, they lined up quietly, hugged Gwen's knees, and filed out with their teacher.

The next class, sixth graders, was one that Gwen worried about. They were difficult students whom she found very difficult to motivate. The students filed in noisily and settled at round tables. Gwen followed the same format—ten minutes to review what they'd do, ten minutes to check out a book, ten minutes to engage in a lesson. She spent a good deal of her time waiting for quiet and disciplining troublesome students. Gwen roamed the room, reminding them to be quiet and moving those who were disrupting others.

She rang a bell to signal that it was time for the lesson, which focused on how they wanted to be remembered as a class by their elementary school. Gwen lectured to the class about a responsibility frame, a technique out of their critical thinking curriculum. The students were clearly uninterested. Gwen stopped repeatedly to ask for their attention.

Everyone was drained by the time they left. Gwen bent over in frustration to pick up pencil shavings and sunflower seeds sprinkled on the floor under one of the desks. "These are Darren's. I know it for a fact. But I'm not sure it's worth a fight."

The school psychologist came in to use the phone in the library office. Gwen winced in frustration again. There was no other phone in the school for teachers to use, because they were not allowed to use the phone in the office. As a result, Gwen was constantly prevented from using her own office while other teachers closed the door to make calls.

Two more classes filed in and followed much the same format as the earlier two, checking books in and out and a brief lesson. A class of fourth graders from the gifted classroom planned a project to make videotaped advertisements. A class of third graders watched an old filmstrip.

Jane came in to take her turn at teaching in the library. She and Gwen discussed the fact that they had $2,400 to spend before the end of the month.

Gwen ate lunch in the large, cheery faculty room. She and the other teachers got to talking about how much more difficult teaching had become as a result of all the family problems and disruptions in home life. The school secretary came in to tell Gwen that Child Protective Services would be there in an hour about a suspected abuse case. Gwen would have to be present during the hearings as the principal designee, because the principal was out of the building.

After lunch, Gwen was released to fulfill her IST responsibilities. Her leadership role had been created by the superintendent, who believed that the role would reduce teacher isolation while increasing teachers' instructional skills. The roles had not been well received by the teachers, but the administration had held firm on them. Each Instructional Support Teacher was selected by the principal in the building. The ISTs had all received training in "Instructional Theory Into Practice" from Dr. Madeline Hunter, who had worked in the district for many years.

Vivian, Gwen's principal, believed that the roles were very successful and said that she had observed some very good results in classrooms where teachers had worked with Gwen. Vivian indicated that Gwen conducted five observations, including feedback sessions, each week. Though Vivian occasionally asked Gwen to work with a particular teacher, they never discussed Gwen's interactions with the teachers. Vivian felt that confidentiality was critical for the teachers' trust levels. She noted that she had worked long and hard to build Gwen's credibility among the staff.

Gwen and I quietly entered a third-grade classroom. The students were playing a game in which they solved a problem and had to race up to the teacher's desk with the right answer. The kids were wild, but working. After calling for quiet, the teacher moved to a timed math quiz. He yelled "Stop!" after a few minutes, and the students moaned and groaned. He then had the students take out their math books. "If you want to do this in class, you can, but you'll have to do it quietly. If you can't be quiet, you'll have to read the book by yourselves." At this point, Gwen, who had been taking notes unobtrusively in the back of the room, put a note on his desk and we left. The observation had lasted approximately eight minutes.

Next we went to the Art Room where Gwen had scheduled a feedback session with the art teacher, who had recently transferred from the community college to the elementary level. They talked for ten minutes about a class Gwen had observed the week before. Gwen indicated that the teacher used her time well, that she had all of the students involved by having them hold up their hands to indicate that they understood what she was doing. The art teacher noted, "I have them do that so I can understand where they are, and so I can watch those kids. I promised them that if they give me a signal, I won't call them on it if it's wrong. I just want them to participate." Gwen also indicated that she might have extended the lesson by connecting what the children were doing to other cultures. They concluded by visiting about their personal lives. The teacher seemed most appreciative of Gwen's feedback.

We stopped outside another doorway. The children in the room were on all fours in a circle, heads down, bottoms up. It was difficult to locate the teacher in the midst of the group. They were studying a box turtle. Gwen veered away from the doorway before entering and explained that ITIP worked best with direct, teacher-centered instruction because she had to take verbatim notes on what the teacher did and said. The turtle lesson was not as appropriate. We called on another class before Gwen had to go attend to the child abuse hearing.

When she returned to the library, she prepared for the next day's assembly. Among her other leadership responsibilities were running all the school's assemblies, coordinating the building's testing program, and planning the spring teas. She felt very fragmented and unable to spend as much time with the teachers as she would have liked. At the end of the day, she was also in charge of the buses; grabbing a few signs and her coat, she flew out to the playground to get the kids lined up in front of the right buses.

As the buses left the grounds, teachers began filing into the library for a faculty meeting. Friends clustered around tables, and everyone chatted quietly. Vivian, the principal, chaired the meeting, which was primarily a discussion about the pros and cons of student awards. The meeting ended with reminders about guarding keys, earthquake drills, and the spring fun run sponsored by the PTA.

After the meeting, Gwen returned to her office to straighten things up and to prepare for the next day. She left at approximately 5:00 p.m.

Gwen's Colleagues

Of the four people interviewed at Gwen's school, all were supportive of Gwen as a person. Two were supportive of her position, while two others were adamantly opposed to it.

Those who supported the position appreciated the opportunity to talk about their teaching with someone else. One of them hoped that her own good ideas could be shared via Gwen with other faculty members. Both of them indicated that they had had some very good discussions with Gwen about teaching, although one noted that those conversations were never about ITIP.

Those opposed to the IST position believed that it increased their class size, that it did not improve the quality of their instruction, or that it was an administrative support position. They were angry because they had not been consulted about the role and had little idea what Gwen did with her time or how the information Gwen gained from classroom observation was used.

Mary Jones: A Reflective Teacher Leader

Mary taught in an experimental project in a large middle school in the northwestern United States. At the time of the study, she was just completing the first year of the project in which she and her colleague, Barbara, team-taught 57 heterogeneously mixed sixth graders. They had the students for one-half of the school day and were responsible for math, science, English, social studies and drug and alcohol education. The curriculum was integrated along thematic lines. They had added

35

computer instruction after they gained access to sixteen computers. No students were pulled out of class for remedial or extra services; all specialists came to them. The women shared two rooms divided by a moveable wall that could be pulled shut when they wished to work in smaller groups.

Mary and Barb had designed this program to provide a demonstration center for other teachers in their building and across their district. Both of them had previously held full-time leadership positions which they did not believe worked satisfactorily. The administrators in their district and in their building were completely supportive of the project and had helped them to get set up and to secure the resources they needed in order to work.

Mary arrived at school at 7:00 a.m.—much earlier than usual—in order to get set up for the day prior to attending a staff meeting. She moved around her room checking on the students' things, placing papers on their desks with words of encouragement written in brightly colored pens. She wrote the beginning assignment on the overhead and moved with Barbara down to the grade-level meeting which had replaced many of the whole faculty meetings.

As people sauntered in slowly, the teachers began to discuss the end-of-the-year field trip to the local zoo. They debated whether they should have sack lunches or a barbecue, whether they should walk the students around the lake after lunch or just return to school, whether they should do worksheets or some kind of activity. The predominant tone was negative.

Eventually Mary, Barbara, and another woman took responsibility for contacting the parents, for organizing slides of African animals, and for organizing activities to be done while at the zoo. The tone was chilly, as the staff was clearly divided between those who constantly advocated for students and those who wanted to do as little as possible. Mary left feeling indignant about the other teachers' responses and attitudes.

Students were waiting outside of her room. She let them

in, pulled the dividing wall shut, and turned on the overhead, which read:

Good morning.

Write: How dialogical reasoning (both sides) is different from my-side reasoning. Which is better? Why? Write neatly and put your name on the paper.

Thank you.

As the students settled in and began to write, Mary used the time to greet students, to listen to their news, and to accept work. She posted a list of due dates on the board and then had the students share what they had written with students near them. She gave them time to revise what they had written to make their own work stronger. She then went over the agenda for the day. They would have one-and-a-half hours of project time—integrated learning time.

The students were studying immigration and had been working on a computer simulation following an Irish family to the United States. In addition, they had completed their own family trees and traced their relatives' journeys to the United States. They had prepared budgets, created family crests with Logo, and studied the countries from which their own families came. Several of the students were recent immigrants—from Cambodia, Iran, and Italy. She reminded them of what still had to be done.

Two boys pushed the wall back and the two classrooms of children quickly mixed and paired up into groups of two and three or four. Several groups raced to the computers to make sure that they got on right away. One willowy little girl sat down to read *Sweet Valley High;* completely engrossed, she did not move for the rest of the project time. An interracial group of boys—two Blacks, an Asian, and one White—pushed four desks together and proceeded to work on their math. One of the boys went to the cutter and sliced paper into fractional segments which they needed to work with. As they began to work, they sang "I'm a

Little Teapot" and laughed while doing the motions. No inhibitions.

Another minuscule girl with long, brown braids worked with a tall Asian girl to get their computer partner, Mike, to work with them. Kittie had secured the computer and was insistent that he come and help. He ignored them until her persistence wore him down. As he grinned and moved with them to the computer, Kittie cheerfully rattled off what they had to do.

Two other boys worked at a computer together, trying to figure out the Logo exercises in the package that Barb had prepared for them. Other groups of students worked with the math specialist in the center of the room. Others sat on the floor in clumps, using resource books to get information for reports. The room hummed and buzzed while Mary and Barbara moved slowly from group to group, giving advice, answering questions, offering encouragement.

Seven teachers and a central office administrator from a neighboring district came in to visit. They were interested in interdisciplinary teaching and wished to observe and to ask questions. Mary and Barb sent them around the room to visit with students. Later Mary answered questions while Barb worked with the students.

During recess, the students played just outside their room so that Mary and Barb could keep an eye on them; to keep the students for four subjects, they had given up their duty-free recesses. Three student teachers came into the room and talked with Barb and Mary about the lessons they would be teaching after recess.

Mary and Barb called the students back together, had them switch sides, and pulled the wall shut. Mary repeated the morning's assignment with this group. While the student teacher prepared her notes, her university supervisor settled into the back of the room to observe. Mary remarked that the supervisor had a very restrictive checklist that guided her observations so she never had the opportunity to watch what the students were doing. Mary sat in the back of the room to collect information on the students as the student teacher hesitantly began the lesson. Mary made some notes but quickly took a cue from the student teacher to resume working with the class.

Mary reviewed with the students what they had to do, peeked through the wall, and opened it up for another forty-minute project time. All the student teachers and Mary and Barb worked with the students. Shortly before lunch, Mary called the entire room back to order and asked the students to write for a few minutes about how they used their project time. The students handed their papers to any of the teachers as they trooped out to lunch. The sudden quiet was unsettling.

At lunch, Mary, Barb, and the student teachers sat apart from the rest of the faculty and discussed the lessons the student teachers presented. They discussed one student who had a great deal of emotional difficulty and wondered how best to support him. They called the principal over to tell him they thought the child had suicidal tendencies, and they spent the rest of the time determining the best possible strategies.

After lunch, Mary, Barbara, and the student teachers were joined in the classroom by a university professor with whom they had been collaborating in the evaluation of their experimental project. After a jovial exchange, they determined how to prepare for the post-test data gathering and the final qualitative data gathering which was about to be completed. Procedures set, they established the dates for a working weekend after the data had been analyzed by the professor. The group would then determine how best to modify their program based on the information they gained. The weekend group would include a central office administrator, another professor, and the two teachers.

The two women then sat down for twenty-minute private debriefing sessions with the student teachers, during which they shared their notes with them. Mary reassured her student teacher that there was no one right way to teach and that teaching was extremely complex, requiring small steps, patience and a love of children. The student teacher left feeling very good about her first attempts at teaching.

Mary and Barb flew out to their cars to rush to the Central Office to meet with their colleagues who had maintained the IST leadership positions which they had held previously. The purpose of the meeting was to enable the two women to summarize their experiences for the rest of the group. They talked about the benefits of their partnership, about how they shared responsibility for everything that happened in the classroom and tried to reach consensus on everything they did. They told about the long hours they had put in to develop an integrated curriculum, because none had existed. They talked about the difficulty they had had in dealing with four of the students who did not work well during class, the demands of working with three student teachers, and the work of coordinating the many visitors who were interested in watching, most of whom came from districts outside their own. Finally, they talked about the discomfort they felt amongst their own staff members, only two of whom had used the center. The conversation was deep and thoughtful.

Several of the specialists noted that they did not want to go back to the classroom because it was so much work. "If you value students to the very highest level of your being," Mary responded, "then you have to behave in these ways. You have to try to find new ways that work." It was nearly 5:30 when the group dispersed.

Mary's Colleagues

Only three colleagues were interviewed at Mary's school; the local association representative divided her time between two buildings and no suitable time could be found for an interview. The remaining three were all supportive of Mary as a person. While they all understood that Mary and Barbara were experimenting with a demonstration classroom, two were unclear about how that impacted their own classrooms. One of the teachers was blatantly angry; she felt that Mary and Barb were given the lion's share of the resources and of the administrators' attention while the rest of the teachers were ignored. She was unclear about the purpose of the project and felt that the rest of the staff needed more information to understand the purpose and the benefit of a demonstration room.

IDENTIFYING THE
COLLABORATIVE RELATIONSHIPS

In their attempts to "lead" colleagues to new kinds of teaching, each of these teachers was engaged in a number of collaborative relationships. Ted collaborated with visiting teachers, teachers who worked for Talking Mountain, and teachers who took his course. Gwen collaborated with Jane and with the teachers she visited in her building and then with the teachers from around the district who took her course. Mary collaborated with Barb, with teachers who visited, with the student teachers, and with university professors, among others.

These various collaborations seemed confusing at first, each different and unique, yet all of them running together and overlapping. However, on further examination, they sorted out into three distinct categories. Ted mentored other teachers, both those in his school who had been hired by Talking Mountain to teach in his high school, and those who took the courses he taught for teachers from around the country. Mary, in her original IST role, functioned as a mentor to the teachers who requested her services as well as to student teachers. Gwen mentored those teachers she observed in the use of ITIP.

Gwen was engaged in another kind of collaboration with Jane. She and Jane shared responsibility for the library and, in order to cope with the work load, divided up the labor. Ted and his fellow Talking Mountain teachers divided up the labor for their third-period class, in that one took responsibility for those students doing writing projects, while another worked with students interested in radio production, and the third worked with students interested in music. Barbara and Mary occasionally

41

divided up the labor for the development of a particular lesson and for working with visitors during class time. Barb focused on computer lessons; Mary was more likely to generate the writing lesson plans.

Mary and Barbara shared a third kind of collaborative relationship. They shared responsibility for the demonstration classroom, the student teachers, and their students. Rather than dividing up the labor, which they did at times, they chose to work together. They spent many hours planning together. Sometimes, each of them would go home and brainstorm ideas for the next unit or for dealing with a student or a student teacher, after which they got together and worked toward a plan both of them could accept. This required more time but ensured a shared philosophy and a consistency that they believed they needed.

Each of these collaborative relationships—mentoring, division of labor, and partnering—creates a different set of dynamics between the collaborating parties. Each requires particular kinds of working relationships, derives power and authority from various sources, and establishes particular kinds of leadership opportunities. Each offers different kinds of incentives, and each defines teacher leadership slightly differently. Consideration of each will help us to understand the differences before returning to the original questions my teaching friends and I generated about teacher leadership.

Mentoring

A mentor, by definition, is an experienced and trusted counselor. In this role, the teacher leaders were to help their colleagues hone their instructional skills or to expand their repertoires. Such a role assumes a hierarchical relationship—that the mentor has expertise worth sharing and that the colleagues recognize that expertise and believe that it will benefit them. It also assumes that they trust the mentor, that the mentor trusts them. Mentoring also requires that teachers have regular time to work together so that they can build trust and a strong relationship. The mentoring relationship involves modeling, discussing, and observing.

In Ted's case, the Talking Mountain teachers recognized Ted's expertise and trusted him. The teachers he worked with took the courses because they had heard of Ted and wanted to learn more from such a successful teacher. His colleagues in his building respected him and trusted him, but did not necessarily believe that his philosophy was appropriate for them. Ted shared a planning period with the Talking Mountain teachers, had time to interact with teachers who took his course during class and during the Network Outreach meetings, but did not have any time to work with his colleagues in his own school. Ted frequently talked about how exhausting it was to have to mentor so many people. He occasionally felt as if he were floundering himself, and that the mentoring role assumed that he had more expertise than he really did, that he always understood what was going on.

The situation in Gwen's school was quite different. Two of the teachers I interviewed did not trust her role. They believed that it was associated with some sort of administrative prerogative and did not know how Gwen used the information she gained in their classrooms with Vivian, the principal. Three of the colleagues did not believe that ITIP, the instructional focus of Gwen's mentoring, would improve their instruction. They claimed that it was overly simplistic and did not address the problems they were experiencing in their classrooms, problems of student motivation, diverse skills, lack of preparation time. Two of her colleagues stated that, while it was helpful to have Gwen in their room to talk about teaching, they seldom talked about ITIP. One shared that Gwen was helpful solving space problems, while the other noted that she hoped her own most successful techniques would be shared through Gwen with others.

Several people noted that Gwen had less teaching experience than they did and, as a result, it was hard to feel that she had a great deal to offer. Gwen did have time to work with other teachers, but that time was frequently eaten up by additional administrative tasks which the principal assigned to her. Furthermore, the teachers had been told by the administration that Gwen "would be coming into their rooms" and that they were expected to cooperate. There had been no negotiations between the teachers and Gwen about when and how Gwen would visit or how they would structure their exchanges. Gwen reflected on her sense that she was sometimes successful, sometimes not:

> There are days when I really think I've helped someone to think something through. Then I feel great. There are other days when I'm not sure that my observations have been helpful—I can't tell whether the teacher is appreciative or just polite. Then, there are other days when the teacher argues with me or clearly doesn't agree with my approach, and then I feel like it would be better to have my own classroom full time. And on the days when I spend all my time arranging teas or assemblies, I want to pull my hair out. While I'm pretty good at that kind of organizational stuff, because I like order, I'd rather work with the teachers.

Mary talked about her role as a mentor to the student teachers. She hoped that in their exchanges she would convince them that there was not a single way to approach school problems, and she encouraged them to develop their own philosophies and approaches. The student teachers—much younger—recognized Mary's and Barb's expertise and felt fortunate to be in their program.

On the other hand, Mary and Barb had restructured their teacher leadership roles because they did not think that they served their colleagues very well. Their IST position as originally conceived was designed so that they would mentor other teachers in the development of a broader teaching repertoire. The demonstration center was designed to foster a kind of mentoring relationship where other teachers could come in and watch, critique, and ask questions, where Mary and Barb determined the kinds of instructional techniques they wanted to demonstrate. So far, only one teacher in the building had chosen to observe, and she was very angry. She claimed that she couldn't tell what was going on in there, and that they had simply managed to gain a lot of resources and a half day of teaching on a full salary. Mary had time to work with her colleagues in that she had two planning periods. Most of the extra time was spent developing the curriculum for the demonstration classroom or working with teachers from other buildings.

Mentors "lead" their colleagues by sharing expertise. There are incentives in mentoring for both parties. For the mentors, the act of explaining is growth-producing in that they learn more about what they do by constant examination. For the colleagues, mentoring is beneficial in that they gain some support in an otherwise very isolated profession. The hope is that those mentored will change their practices to incorporate the suggestions of the mentors.

Division of Labor

Collaborative relationships that divide the labor are common in bureaucratic organizations like school districts, which have numerous tasks to accomplish and limited human resources. Division of labor suggests that the primary goal of the partnership is to accomplish the task—whatever that might be—and to get it done effectively. A conventional school structure is itself a division of labor, but tasks are assigned by a manager. It assumes that the partners have some expertise which they will apply to those tasks they know the most about, and that work can be accomplished in a rational and orderly fashion. It requires that people work together to determine the scope of task, and that colleagues agree about who will do what. It does not require that the partners agree on how things are done, or that they share the same values and feelings about the work. It is based on an efficiency principle (many hands make light work) and an effectiveness principle (each person will do those tasks for which he or she has the greatest expertise).

Gwen and Ted provide the clearest examples. Gwen and Jane divided up the labor of running the library. Gwen fulfilled her half of the library responsibilities without ever consulting with Jane. Neither of them asked the other for a critique of their individual efforts. When they disagreed about how something should be done, the person who held primary responsibility for the task was responsible for deciding. Both felt the benefits of working together, without having to invest a good deal of their personal time in reaching consensus. They met regularly on Friday afternoons to deal with things that cropped up.

Ted and his colleagues divided up the labor of teaching a large class. Each took responsibility for students interested in a particular discipline—music, writing, or videography. They spent more time sharing—they met together every day for one period—because they had ongoing responsibilities with the students. They benefitted from their division of labor in that at least one of them generally had rapport with a particular student in need of help. At the same time, they seldom talked together about what they actually did in their respective lessons on music, writing, or videography.

The incentives for engaging in this kind of collaboration are imbedded in the ability to get a good deal accomplished in a shorter time with greater effectiveness. Isolation for teachers is reduced, without necessarily challenging their autonomy or causing them to share attitudes, beliefs and practices with others. When collaborating in division of labor, the parties involved are not necessarily influenced to change common practices by those with whom they work.

Leadership—moving others to new practices—is less obvious in a division of labor collaboration. In this case, each participant has the opportunity to share personal expertise where required but does not necessarily affect the practices of others. While the opportunity to influence others exists, given the regular time scheduled for collaboration, each team member takes leadership for his/her respective task and accomplishes the task according to individual preference and judgment.

Partnering

Partners generally choose to join together in some mutually interesting effort and agree to share equally in the work, the benefits and the risks. Partnering requires more time than either mentoring or division of labor in that the partners agree to agree on as much as possible. It assumes that the partners have comparable skill and an equal investment in the project or tasks. It requires that the partners learn skills of consensus-building and that they give up their personal autonomy. It requires a good deal of trust between the partners.

Mary and Barb were the only two who engaged in the more equal relationship of partnering. At the outset of their mutual relationship, they determined what kind of classroom they wanted to create and then determined that they would attempt to work together to reach consensus on as many decisions as they could. They believed that this was important because they wanted to present a consistent and united front to both students and visitors. It required that they spend far more time working together, since they had to agree on everything they wanted to do. Mary described the relationship:

> I've had to give up a lot this year, old ideas I've had about the way things ought to be done. Some of them I've really struggled for, too—fought with Barb to get. In the long run, I've learned that there are far more ways to skin an educational cat than I ever imagined. At first it was important to me that I got to do things my way. Now I can see that we aren't competing—my ideas against hers—but trying to figure out the best way to support the students and visiting teachers. We'd end up modifying both of our ideas in the long run. It's been a tough lesson, but this has also been my best year. I have learned a lot. Barb has helped me to understand that kids can do more than one thing at a time. She has confirmed my beliefs that even middle school kids work together better when they collaborate. I feel more professional than I ever have before.

The agreement to partner meant that Mary and Barbara

47

had to hammer out their beliefs, their values, and their goals for the course. It also meant that they had to agree on every lesson plan, curricular unit, scheduling arrangement, request for visits, disciplinary action for kids. They had to agree that they shared equal responsibility for everything that happened in the room, including the screw-ups. Partnering also implied that they trusted each other and believed that they held equal expertise. They had two planning periods per day to work together, but generally met at school a full hour before the bell rang and generally spent an evening or a weekend morning together. They were both on regular teaching salaries, and were not compensated for the additional time. Outsiders who visited the room were impressed at how smoothly the two women seemed to handle so much activity and diversity.

The incentives to partner are that isolation is significantly reduced and that partnering is at once confirming and growth-producing. Each partner must, at the same time, explain her beliefs and practices, examine them, and consider those of her partner(s) as well. Partners believe that they make better decisions because they gain both creativity and objectivity in their decision-making when more than one person participates.

The relationship between partnering and leadership is again less traditional. Rather than one leader influencing others, both parties "lead" each other to new practices. Because the partners must agree on teaching strategies and materials, both will try new things. Partners "lead" each other when building new curriculum or trying new instructional techniques.

THE POWER BASE IN COLLABORATIVE RELATIONSHIPS

In our beginning discussions we determined that teacher leadership required some power base, some source of authority that allows leaders to influence others. We examined each of these types of collaborative relationships in an attempt to determine where each derives its power.

In 1959, French and Raven described a taxonomy of power sources that has proven influential. According to their work, there are five sources of power:

1. Reward power: People gain reward power when they have the ability to reward their colleagues.

2. Coercive power: People gain coercive power when they have the ability to punish their colleagues.

3. Legitimate Power: People gain legitimate power when there is an internalization of common norms and values between the parties involved.

4. Referent power: People gain referent power by virtue of their association with someone else others respect.

5. Expert power: People gain expert power when others perceive them to have valuable expertise.

Obviously, successful mentors have expert power. The important point, for our purposes, is *who recognizes* the expertise of the leader. If, as in Gwen's case, the principal determines that she has expertise worth sharing, her position might be foiled if her colleagues don't agree. Mary's expertise was determined by the central office administrators for the original IST position. When she and Barb recreated their position, they gained the approval of the administration, but did not check with their colleagues to see if the expertise they hoped to offer would be useful. Ted was recognized as an expert by those teachers who chose to take his course and chose to join the outreach networks. As a result, he did not feel the frustration the other two did.

Gwen was given coercive power. Teachers in her building had been told that they "would participate" in the IST program by the administration. While there was no explicit discussion of the kind of punishment that might be meted out if they did not cooperate, several of the teachers did not trust Gwen because they did not know what she did with the information she gained in their classrooms. As a result, they engaged in overt compliance with her and then, frequently, covertly dismissed the position as useless. The principal gave Gwen the authority, but it was diminished by the lack of teacher compliance.

Two examples of legitimate power are illuminated in the three cases. Barb and Mary collaboratively determined their purposes and established their common values. Together they were equals in their partnership to create a better, more powerful classroom for students. Both gained from the expertise of the others and at the same time, believed that they were able to use their own expertise. The teachers who chose to participate in Ted's courses and in the Outreach Network were given the message that once the mentoring relationship was finished, they might form partnerships with other like-minded teachers by participation in the network activities, that their own expertise was valuable.

Referent power also existed within these collaborations. Teachers who chose to teach courses with Ted after engaging in their own experiments were frequently perceived to have referent power, in that their association with him, and his request that they work together, sanctioned their work. In this case, this worked to their advantage, since most of the teachers who took the class did so because they believed in Ted.

Recognition of the power source in teacher leadership positions is important as leaders need some source of authority to influence their colleagues. Real collaboration must be consensual. The nature of the power is determined by each individual in his or her relation to the leader; what a principal perceives as expert power may be seen as reward or coercive power by others. The source must be perceived as authentic by both the leaders and the led if any significant gains are to be made.

ANSWERS TO QUESTIONS

Gradually, from our examination of these teacher leaders, I began to understand that teacher leaders are engaged in three distinctly different collaborative relationships—mentoring, division of labor, and partnering. Each cast a slightly different light on the definition of teacher leadership and how it is practiced. In addition, each type of relationship carried with it a particular source of power and authority.

From these realizations, I returned to the original set of questions: If leadership is the ability to lead others to change and improve their practice, and if teachers hope to change practice through collaboration with their colleagues, what kind of collaboration produces the most effective kinds of leadership? Do existing teacher leadership positions provide collaborative opportunities which influence a change in practice? How does this relate to the current national call for teacher leadership positions? An examination of each of these questions will provide some clarity.

What is the relationship between collaboration and leadership?

It seems clear that collaborative opportunities become effective leadership when the collaboration influences the behavior of others. When Ted mentored other teachers in his courses, and they approached both their curriculum and their instruction quite differently as a result, he had fulfilled a leadership function. When Jane and Gwen divided up the responsibility for running the library and each of them carried out their tasks in isolation from the other, neither was influenced to change, although they spent some time each Friday in actual collaborative work. Their division of labor relationship did not fulfill a leadership function. When Mary and Barb sat down to plan a unit on immigration, combining their ideas about how the unit should be taught and assessed, they were each influenced by the ideas of the other; each changed her practices to incorporate the ideas and expertise of the other. Thus, they fulfilled a leadership role for each other and engaged in constant collaboration as well.

Obviously, none of these collaborative relationships is as pure or as simple as suggested by these examples. Ted frequently

51

remarked that he learned as much from the people he was mentoring as they did from him. Jane noted that Gwen had helped her to be much more organized in the running of the library as they talked over what had to be done. And Mary and Barb at times hung onto their own beliefs and practices when one was not convinced by the other. Nevertheless, mentoring and partnering seemed to have greater potential to influence and change practice than did division of labor.

What kinds of collaborative relationships provide the greatest opportunity to influence a change in practice?

Existing leadership roles do seem to provide the opportunity for teachers to collaborate, but they do not always seem designed to lead others to change their current practices. We concluded that the ability to change practice was heavily influenced by the source of the power. In the cases where the source of the power did not come from those who were to be influenced by the leader, the potential for change significantly diminished. For instance, when Ted was perceived to be an expert by teachers who voluntarily took his courses, his ability to influence their practice increased. In his own building, where he had no formal authority and where he was well respected but not a famous teacher—where his expert power was diminished—his ability to influence others diminished. When Gwen was given the authority to go into other teachers' classrooms by the principal, but not invited by the teachers, her ability to influence practice was all but nonexistent. Mary's attempt to influence the practice of the other teachers in her building in the demonstration center also failed, because her colleagues had not been involved in the decision-making about her role or about the center and therefore did not perceive her role as legitimate. On the other hand, when two teachers like Mary and Barb entered into a mutually agreed upon partnership, each influenced the practice of the other and shared a legitimate source of power in that they had collaboratively determined their aims and beliefs. We came to agree that for teacher leadership positions to work, the source of power and authority had to be granted to the leaders by their colleagues—those they wished to lead.

How do these leadership positions relate to the current call for leadership positions for teachers in the national reports?

The national reports suggested staged career ladders and hierarchical steps, which involved greater mentoring roles for experienced teachers. We concluded that such roles might prove beneficial if those to be mentored had some influence in the design of the role and the relationship. We noted, however, that the positions suggested in the reports generally did not include partnering, and that partnering was perhaps the most appealing of the three kinds of collaboration because it was less hierarchical and provided more equal incentives for both parties.

The examination of these three leadership positions suggested that these current roles are less effective than they could be when the teachers whose practice might be influenced have not been involved in the creation, design or evaluation of the positions. Until that happens, teacher leaders are unlikely to have broad influence with their peers.

CLARIFYING COLLABORATION

As a result of the effort to better understand teacher leadership and its relationship to collaboration, I came away with several clarifications central to the building of more powerful leadership positions for teachers.

1. Teacher leadership assumes that teachers have the ability to influence their peers to change common practice on behalf of better learning for students. Many teachers do not want to leave the classroom to do that, nor do they want to undertake management functions. Rather, they would like to focus on those issues that influence student learning.

2. In order for teachers to be able to influence their peers, they must have a legitimate source of power. Colleagues to be served by teacher leaders should be involved in the design of

such roles and the selection of those to fill them. Only with such authorization will the leaders actually have the potential to change practice.

3. Teachers are interested in leadership opportunities that allow them to collaborate with their colleagues. Some collaborative relationships are more likely to change practice than others. Mentoring and partnering relationships require those involved to examine their existing practices in light of another's expertise or suggestions.

4. Collaborative relationships provide different kinds of incentives—some more powerful than others—and these should be considered by all involved when designing new opportunities.

Given the valuable information and insights gained from Ted, Gwen, and Mary, I was personally convinced of the power of collaboration as a means for bringing about more potent classrooms, and more powerful schools. The year after I spent time with them, I found myself thinking about how difficult it had been for me in my traditional high school setting to learn about other approaches when I only saw my colleagues for the twenty-minute lunch gulp. I had learned enough new strategies from visiting Ted's and Gwen's and Mary's classrooms to last ten years, and I wanted to try some of them out. So I found myself a partner in a nearby elementary school and a lively group of fourth graders who seemed quite happy to work with two teachers instead of just one.

We divided up some of the labor: I did the drama lessons connected to her art lessons. Ms. Hong did the math lessons to generate a budget, while we worked on a book for children at the local hospital. Mostly we partnered, taking shared responsibility for everything we were trying to do. We argued; we lobbied for our own best ideas. Occasionally, though I don't like to admit it, I sulked a little, and once or twice she let me have it. We tried a number of new strategies, many of which we would each have put in the good idea file if we had not had the prompting of our partner. We celebrated when something worked well and analyzed when it didn't. Most importantly, we both grew enormously, while we watched our students do things we never would have believed they could do.[1]

FOOTNOTE

1. A number of teachers reacted to these ideas and helped me to clarify my thinking. They were from the Puget Sound Educational Consortium in Seattle; the North Clackamas School District in Oregon; the NEA Mastery In Learning Project; the Matsushita Foundation projects in San Diego and Santa Fe; and several member schools in the Coalition of Essential Schools. I am indebted to them for struggling through tough issues and for their willingness to collaborate.

REFERENCES

Bacharach, S. B. 1986. *The learning workplace: The conditions and resources of teaching.* Washington, D.C.: National Education Association.

Bass, B. M., ed. 1981. *Stogdill's handbook of leadership: A survey of theory and research.* Revised and expanded edition. New York: Free Press.

Carnegie Foundation for the Advancement of Teaching. 1986. *A nation prepared: Teachers for the 21st century.* Report of the Task Force on Teaching as a Profession. New York: The Foundation.

French, J. R. P., and Raven, B. 1959. The bases of social power. In *Studies in social power,* ed. D. Cartwright. Ann Arbor: University of Michigan, Institute for Social Research. Cited in Bass, 1981.

Holmes Group. 1986. *Tomorrow's teachers: A report of the Holmes Group.* East Lansing, Mich.: The Group.

McLaughlin, M. W., and Yee, S. M. 1988. School as a place to have a career. In *Building a professional culture in schools,* ed. A. Lieberman, 23–44. New York: Teachers College Press.

Wasley, P. A. 1991. *Teacher leadership: Problems, paradoxes and possibilities.* New York: Teachers College Press.

Chapter 2

EMPOWERMENT THROUGH LEADERSHIP: IN THE TEACHERS' VOICE

by Carolyn Fay

Empowerment and leadership are explored from the perspectives of teacher leaders in three schools engaged in a national school reform project. The teachers describe their leadership role—its demands, how it was perceived and received by colleagues, its relationship to the teachers' instructional mission, and its distinction from administrative roles and traditional uses of power. The study of teacher leadership should lead to the construction of new paradigms for leadership in schools. Professional development programs need to provide leadership development for practicing and aspiring teacher leaders.

Increasing recognition of the inherent leadership qualities in classroom teachers has led to deeper study of teacher leadership and the potential for teacher responsibility and authority in shaping climate and curriculum in their schools.

In fact, teacher leadership is a strong indicator of one of the more recent educational reform imperatives—teacher empowerment (Fay 1989). These reform imperatives have evolved from "first order" change, concerned with control and regulations, to a second order of "new goals, structures and roles" (Cuban 1988, p. 344).

Many reformers state that teacher empowerment is essential to this second order change, often termed school restructuring. And yet, empowered teachers are not generally

57

found in American public schools as they are structured today, despite research demonstrating the importance of teacher empowerment and autonomy and despite attempts to include teachers at the decision-making table (Rice 1987).

Indeed, Maeroff (1988b) points out that the "centrality of the teacher's role in determining what happens in schools . . . is often ignored in the recommendations for improving schools" (p. 1). And Boyer (1988) states that today's teachers may have gained in competency and responsibility, but they lack "empowerment to shape curricula, programs and policy" (p. 66). Frymier (1989) goes further, describing teachers as "neutered" by the bureaucratic routinization of teaching and learning that has grown out of administrative attempts to control schools as places with teachers as deskilled workers and students as uniform products.

Teacher Leadership and Conditions for Empowerment

For their empowerment, teachers must achieve "status, knowledge, and access to decision making" (Maeroff 1988a, p. 473) if they are to be able to directly address matters of teaching and learning, still most teachers' primary concerns (Johnston and Germinario 1986).

It may well be that genuine teacher empowerment depends upon practitioners themselves determining the very conditions that foster their empowerment by developing new beliefs about their ability to lead colleagues in school change. "Involving people authentically in dealing with their own professional lives . . . real participation by teachers reflecting their vision of participation" is one way Ann Lieberman describes teacher empowerment (Brandt 1989). By actively creating their own visions of empowerment and leadership and refusing the imposition of others' versions, teachers will ensure two essentials in expanding their role: appropriateness and ownership.

Leadership roles empower teachers to actualize their professional worth in concrete, fundamental ways: sharing their unique experience and expertise with one another, developing new skills with colleagues for improving their schools, and designing actual roles that both promote these functions and maintain the centrality of their teaching.

Professionalism, Teacher Leadership, and the Bureaucracy

Most discussion of teacher leadership does not attempt to compare, in any way, these new expanded roles with those of typical school administrators. It seems clear that teachers do not see leadership as others traditionally have—as a "higher" place in the organizational hierarchy. Their sense of professionalism keeps their leadership tied directly to what affects their students. "Teachers place high value on their work with students. They do not desire upward movement in the organization . . . into administration" (Devaney 1987, p. 9).

Teachers do indeed want to stay close to their students and each other, and they see administration as distant from both. Further, they are generally uncomfortable with competitive "incentive" plans that reward only a few teachers. School observers have noted that teachers thrive best in an atmosphere of cooperation and collaboration:

> It is hard to detect a groundswell of support from teachers for most of the career-ladder proposals; policy makers . . . and researchers have been the most vocal advocates. The element of competition contained in career-ladder plans may be only one of several reasons for their lukewarm reception from teachers. The "promotion and advancement" vision of career reflected in such plans does not necessarily match teachers' conceptions of career (Little 1988, p. 80).

Teaching is demeaned by a hierarchical viewpoint that terms leaving the classroom as a "promotion." Devaney (1987) stresses the danger of confusing empowerment with rank:

> The objective must be to improve the effectiveness and commitment of all teachers. The lead teacher position must be

59

an organizational and workplace reform, not just a career ladder. Otherwise, it will be resisted by teachers who see the lead teacher as one more person in the hierarchy empowered to tell them what to do and positioned above them on the bureaucratic ladder (p. 16).

Teachers, then, do not confuse their ideas of expanded leadership roles with "rising in the ranks." But others may. Lieberman (1988) warns that "the move to professionalize teaching will inevitably conflict with the bureaucratic orientation of schools and of school people who have held positions of authority in the hierarchy" (p. 649).

But for teachers to realize a new sense of professionalism, traditional bureaucratic structures can no longer serve as governance models. Teacher authority in the substance of school will need to be clearly differentiated from organizational or managerial authority (Erlandson and Bifano 1987).

By gaining autonomy and control of their profession, teachers can transform "the manner in which administrators interact with the teaching staff" (Pratte and Rury 1988, p. 72). Genuine colleagueship between teachers and principals can result, says Barth (1988), when the solitary authority of the principal is replaced with the collective authority of the faculty. School becomes "a community of leaders, a place whose very mission is to insure that students, parents, teachers, and principals all become school leaders in some ways and at some times" (p. 640).

Some educators see teachers as unwilling to take any formal responsibility for school governance. It is difficult, however, even to estimate how many teachers want what kind of decision-making or actual leadership responsibility. It is safe to say that not all teachers are equally desirous or capable of significant participation, nor are all decisions of equal importance to those who do choose to participate. According to Alutto and Belasco (1972), teachers can become saturated with decisional involvement. But the quality and degree of decision making that teachers are asked to do needs further study from the teacher viewpoint. Involving teachers early on before decisions are already made, as Barth (1990) suggests, might change teacher perception that their part in the school decision-making process is a mere rubber-stamp activity, useless to accomplish the kinds of change they see as important and, worse, a waste of their time.

THE STUDY[1]

Both the concept and the language of teacher empowerment sound positive to teacher readers of recent reform literature. All too often, however, the familiar absence of practicing teacher's voices—even in the discussion of their own empowerment—is apparent.

Talking about teachers without talking to them or with them—as if they exist only in the third-person—has been an unfortunately common practice among many educators. But discussing teacher *empowerment* without including teachers as active participants in the dialogue seems so inappropriate as to be ludicrous, when this "power" is so obviously and so intrinsically *theirs,* by virtue of their direct work with students and thus, one would think, theirs to shape and use.

Some teacher leaders clearly have been able and willing to try to forge new roles, responsibilities, and working relationships for themselves. What do they think? What do they and their colleagues say? The only appropriate source, it seemed to me, for determining teachers' perceptions regarding empowerment and leadership roles would be teachers themselves, especially teacher leaders. Thus it was that I determined to go to practicing teachers who were empowered with new leadership roles in their schools, and hear them, in their own words, talk about this form of empowerment and what it meant to them. I was particularly interested in how they combined their teaching role with the newer one of leadership, how one affected the other, and how their expanded roles were viewed by their colleagues.

Participants

Bob McClure of NEA's Mastery In Learning Project (MIL) was aware of my interest in eliciting teachers' viewpoints on teacher empowerment/leadership. We talked about conducting my study in three of the MIL schools and communicated a request for participation in the study to Woodson, Appleton, and Norbridge[2] via the electronic network NEA had set up for the schools in the project. I was happy we got a "yes" from all three for a number of reasons:

I had wanted to interview and observe teachers working at the three levels of elementary, middle/junior high and secondary, to cross urban and suburban lines into rural areas, and to include faculties of differing sizes. The MIL "sample" offered me this opportunity. Appleton Elementary School could be termed small and rural. Norbridge Junior High is mid-sized and located in a small city. And Woodson High School, located in an urban area, is a big complex of various buildings that sprawls over what everyone calls a campus.

Aside from the broad perspective that a national project lent to my inquiry (Mastery In Learning included twenty-six schools across the country), I could also depend on certain conditions in schools with membership in MIL: Voluntary participation of teachers; district commitment and principal's agreement for school involvement; a research base, including teacher assessment of school needs for change efforts; and most important to me, faculty selection of the teacher leadership for the project.

Method

The faculties in each of the three MIL schools I studied had elected colleagues to chair what were called steering committees. Led by this chair (at Norbridge, two teachers were elected as co-chairs), these committees literally steered faculty and staff participation in MIL.

I sent the teacher chairs of each Steering committee a short description of my study's purpose and followed it up with calls to their homes. It made good sense to me to ask these Steering Committee Chairs to be the primary respondents in my inquiry and, further, to select colleagues in their schools who wished to participate in the study by sharing their views on teacher empowerment.

These other teachers—twelve of the teacher leaders' colleagues at the three schools—eventually supplied valuable insights that added texture and color to the stories of those whom they had elected as their leaders. The principals in each of the three schools also agreed to interviews in which they might offer ideas about their own leadership as well as teacher leadership.

I visited each school twice, in the spring and in the fall, spending from twelve to thirty hours in interviews during each of the six visits. I also observed and participated in a number of activities in group settings; these ranged from sitting in on team planning time to attending faculty meetings, from a TGIF gathering of local association reps at a local bar to a crafts fair in a small mountain town, from a school improvement session on a hot Friday afternoon to dinner in the Steering Committee chair's home. Still, in no way would I say I *knew* the schools, or even the teachers that I spent the most time with. What I would say is that we talked as my colleagues at home and I talk— as professionals, as practitioners. That was what I wanted.

Finally, I set three personal guidelines for my study: to acknowledge and honor the gift of teachers' time; to honor respondents' emerging concerns while maintaining the stated focus of the research; and to write a report with an engaging format and style and a sense of real life—one that would do justice to these teachers.

TEACHER LEADERSHIP AT THE MASTERY IN LEARNING SITES

Although all of the teacher leaders at the three MIL sites

employed similar methods and instruments for assessing faculty determination of school need, each used individual interests and skills in leading the project to meet those needs. The focus at each site thus developed in completely different ways. Nevertheless, the MIL teacher leaders experienced a number of similar concerns. What follows are descriptions of the leadership of the MIL Project at the three school sites and of the similarities and differences in the ways their teacher leadership concerns evolved.

Woodson

Woodson is a large urban high school with a seasoned faculty and a heterogeneous student body. As my taxi turned in the driveway that first April morning, the school had already come to life. Students thronged the inner courtyard at the center of the complex, slamming lockers and giving the vending machines a good workout. Teachers finished their coffee as they walked to meet their first period classes.

After the bell rang, I found the main office, looked over the teacher schedule and then walked over to the media center to prepare for my first interview. In the now deserted courtyard, a small band of birds swooped for crumbs left by the morning snackers. Only this rather charming exception kept me from the feeling that I could have been in almost any of the urban secondary settings I have known and worked in. High school commonplaces were alive and well at Woodson. I wondered then what differences there were here, whether I would discover them, and whether newly empowered leadership had made the differences.

MIL Leadership at Woodson

The MIL Project at Woodson superseded an existing school improvement effort which had been system-initiated and administratively directed. Julia, the Woodson Steering Committee Chair, was the school's media center director and had no regular classroom responsibilities; this position, according to her, afforded observations and interactions that gave rise to a view of

64

school need different from what a classroom teacher's might be. This fact and another—Julia had recently completed doctoral studies which had sharpened her interest and skills in research—played important parts in her leadership and faculty response to it.

Reactions to the MIL project and its leadership were mixed from the beginning. Faculty members who had been influential in the earlier school improvement program saw MIL as somewhat of an upstart process, through which a new type of leadership had surfaced and made itself felt. One career teacher, Nathan—who had long functioned at Woodson in various leadership roles—felt he represented other teachers' views when he said:

The MIL process has been manipulated, not only to get things through that they want to do, but to keep out things that they don't want.

An even more fundamental problem, according to Nathan, was the fact that Julia was not a classroom teacher:

There is some dissatisfaction on campus with some of the leadership. The last few years we have had [in leadership of the MIL project] people who have not been in the classroom. There is some resentment on the part of classroom teachers that these people don't understand the classroom any more, that they've got a pretty soft job.

Julia's leadership was hampered, according to Nathan, because she lacked a classroom teacher's viewpoint. Her efforts to bring about change in school climate, student learning styles and governance were fine, he said, but first things first.

Where Does Restructuring Begin?

Nathan stated a variation of a common refrain that I heard over and over again, from teachers at all levels in all three schools. "Restructuring" needs to start at what they consider the

65

heart of teaching—the curriculum:

> I think that trying to involve people is fine, but . . . we are neglecting other areas . . . . Our curriculum is being allowed to drift. We don't have the structure in place in our department to have ongoing curriculum development.

Meanings of "curriculum" vary widely, but, however they define it, most teachers see it as an absolutely vital link between them and their students. Curriculum is what teachers see themselves as most knowledgeable about—and, conversely, what they seldom have any control over. Nathan continued:

> Look at the master schedule. Everybody is plugged into a slot every period of the day, and you are plugged into a slot by yourself. There is nobody but you. Our department is just a bunch of individuals with the chair running around trying to keep us in supplies and that is about it. Curriculum is compiled and passed down by people who are no longer in the classroom [operating] without collegial consensus and support.

Empowerment and Leadership—Different Views

Nathan defined empowerment as "the ability, based on practice and expertise, to make decisions about matters closest to [his] classroom work with students: determining who teaches what, to whom, when and why." All else is secondary, even extraneous. And he sees leadership as a force able to understand:

> The one thing that brings us all together is the student. Somebody somewhere has to sit down and establish policy, and the primary focus has to be the student and the course we want them to run. I think the curriculum has to drive the whole system of education.

Julia did not so much dismiss this central concern of teachers, as she did their approach to it. Her dealings with students in the media center allow her to see needs, she says, that

66

go beyond the curriculum to the students themselves. And classroom teachers are often too mired in content issues to discern these needs, according to her.

One of Julia's tacks as leader was an effort to engage Woodson teachers in reading research. She was confident in this approach: "The surveys I sent out showed [the teachers] had an interest in talking with other teachers about educational issues rather than content areas." Her well-written encapsulations—circulated as "Research Updates"—covered the waterfront: effective schools, motivation, teaching/learning styles, class size, at-risk students, cooperative learning, ability grouping, school culture, homework, dropouts, burnout, technology, etc.

Faculty Decision

The teachers at Woodson were generous in their praise of Julia's ability to go after and compile information that was readable and current and research-based. A good number of them were, in fact, favorable towards the project in general.

However, such positive reactions were not enough to win for her the widespread colleague support essential for successful teacher leadership. Less than two weeks after my first visit to Woodson, the faculty voted against participating for a third year in the MIL project, thereby ending the position of Steering Committee Chair, and in effect, Julia's leadership role in the faculty.

What happened? Was Julia's vision of leadership different from the faculty's? And if so, how?

Leadership Styles

By her own admission, Julia saw leadership more as an individual than a shared endeavor. "Power" is held as a personal utility. Her version depicts the traditional administrator, not a teacher leader:

I've always been a leader. The person who does the work gets the power. If you don't do managerial and even clerical tasks, you lose it. When you do the tasks, you take on the role. To assign it to someone else, you run the risk of not being effective.

Julia's picture has accurate points. However, it lacks an essential sense of leadership, just as the next passage misses the essence of teaching. Both are telling as to the difficulties she experienced in extending her acknowledged capabilities as media specialist/research expert to successful leadership of the faculty. Few career teachers would embrace her following description; a good many might resent it:

Leadership causes quality people to move out. As we excite teachers about their potential [for other responsibilities] they are no longer satisfied with their role in the classroom. Think about it, a better desk, a better chair, a telephone, a clerk, even a secretary. You do not wait for a bell. You don't have to hurt for those kids day after day. I couldn't cope with that pain.

Had Julia measured the intensity of faculty needs more perceptively, she would have probably found that, although research findings were of interest to the teachers, *deeper and closer concerns* existed that had to be dealt with first. Time consuming as it may be, achieving faculty consensus and then leading faculty-initiated change are accomplishable processes. The ability to understand and accept where a faculty stands seems not only helpful but essential for faculty leadership.

Beth, the classroom teacher who was shortly to take over the school leadership role from Julia, saw leadership in a different, more teacher-oriented light.

Wary of aspects of traditional administrative leadership that have long held negative connotations for teachers, Beth wanted no part of "authoritative situations that have to do with power." Her understanding of differences among teachers and the burden of their work is clear:

There is no way you can impose anything on the faculty the

68

way they are working now. We have to improve communication, understand better about adult learning, and increase collegiality and unity. The faculty all have very different philosophies, very different ideas about improvement, and there is a lot of division—about how you handle kids, the teacher-student relationship, and the teacher mission. We've got to accept that and go with it.

With rare sympathy and respect, Beth described certain non-involved faculty, in particular veteran teachers nearing the end of their careers:

Many have been teaching a very long time. Perhaps at their time and in their period they did give a lot, and they have justified it that they are not going to anymore. They have paid their dues. Only a very small percentage of teachers are the kind we see suffering daily, really unhappy. A far larger percentage, maybe just a few years from retirement, are still interested. You can see it when you talk to them. They're still interested in what is going on because they know what is going on still affects them. But they do not want to participate, or "improve" because they are tired, or they just feel they cannot. By tired, I mean they feel like they have paid their dues already.

Beth did not write off these teachers, but acknowledged their value and their right to be recognized for what they have done throughout their careers. She envisions working with them:

You tap their knowledge and experience and give them an opportunity in a forum to just share their ideas. I think it would start like a one-on-one. For example, in my leadership role, I would approach these teachers: "I would really like for you to be involved," and ask them how they might want to contribute, give them options. Maybe I would be too shy, just to come up like that, but maybe getting to know them and then lead into it. I am not sure how I would approach it but [I would find] a way for them to be involved. Everyone has something to offer.

69

Change in Leadership

A new school year had begun when I revisited Woodson. Beth had just assumed her new leadership responsibilities. She called the transition from Julia's leadership "a real difficult time, a very difficult situation" with the faculty divided into two factions. One group wanted to continue the MIL project, another didn't. The faculty voted "about 2/3 against MIL." According to Beth, there was a strong feeling that, because of the way the project had been working, the people who got the benefits were the members of the steering committee, but the faculty as a whole did not directly benefit.

Hardest of all for Beth was weighing the personal impact of the defeat on Julia against the need to respond to the voice of the majority of the faculty.

> I was upset when Julia would not stay involved. She feels I turned on her, and then I was split. I sensed the faculty didn't want it (MIL), and because I was going to have to take the School Improvement Team over, I wanted the faculty to be behind it. Still there was the loss of a tremendous resource. I tried everything to get her to stay with the program, no matter what, but after that [the MIL defeat] she just sent all her material over to me. It is a sad story, because she had done tremendous amounts of things. It was all very emotional.

The transition was otherwise smooth—a tribute to the MIL structure which essentially remained in place, even with a new leader, a return to the School Improvement Team name, and the forming of new committees.

Beth's sense of her own leadership is still being shaped, but one thing is clear—it is grounded in respect for the teachers she serves, and acceptance for healthy differences and disagreement. She is acutely aware of the complexity of meeting the needs of a large group of professionals who have traditionally operated in isolation. One special quandary is the allocation of time for professional development. There is the camp whose members will not leave the classroom for anything or anyone—they see their classroom work not only as top priority but as the only priority. Others feel the need for growth but insist that the district should provide released time; still others prefer activities outside of the school day with their time paid for. Beth has already learned to deal with ambiguity, a skill most leadership theorists call essential:

> The main thing I have learned in the past few months is that last year I was out to get everybody together, and we would all find solutions to all the problems. Now I am doing well if I can get through this year just knowing that I've communicated between all these factions and allow them to feel they have been heard. I think as long as we can communicate our philosophy to each other, we'll know that I am not going to infringe upon each other's feelings.

Leaders Who Continue to Teach

Asked about what makes teacher leadership work, Beth was firm about the need for leaders who are able to continue teaching. Acknowledging the magnitude of the unresolved problem of extra time—or new time—in the teacher day for formal leadership, she still maintained that teacher voice and viewpoint are key, especially if the leadership is to have credibility with the faculty: "We have a faction in this school that really resents leadership by people who are not teachers; I mean, how can you deal with teacher issues if you are not a teacher?" In addition to credibility is the effectiveness arising from the sheer good sense that teachers have about what happens daily in classrooms:

> If you deal with kids on a daily basis, then you know what you're talking about. I don't think anybody else can resolve some of the hot issues that deal with the logistics of how we work with kids. The way they're being resolved by administrative people drives teachers crazy.

71

Power, Leadership, and Management

Beth joins the vast majority of her colleagues in refusing to link traditional power behavior with her ideas of teacher leadership: "Some people just like power, and some feel they have to have it to sort of push things around. I don't get any personal pleasure out of telling people what to do. I don't visualize myself as being higher than anybody else. I'm a quiet leader." She does admit that she is driven by a vision for change. "I know what motivates me—it's my own personal striving for reform in education. I am a real advocate for renewal, and didn't realize how strong I felt about it until I did a lot of reading."

Like many teacher leaders, Beth has taken administrative courses. She finds, as most teachers do, that these courses are not informed by a vision for leading change to meet students' needs, nor are they preparation for what really needs to be done. The stress in her voice reflected the stress between traditional school administration and teachers' ideas of leadership:

> I look at their job descriptions and, oh, they sit there and try, they want to make real improvements for [at-risk kids], but they are so absorbed in managing the school, managing the building, managing, managing. Either manage or get someone else to manage. We need leaders.

Norbridge

It was a cool, grey morning when Kat, a 7th grade home ec teacher, picked me up at my motel. The co-chair of the MIL Steering Committee, she would be one of my primary respondents. We soon drove into the parking lot of Norbridge Junior High, a modern structure, solid and rather somber in appearance. It looked like its conservative midwestern community, which is home to a major research hospital and a branch of a large international corporation. Thus, I wasn't prepared for the riot of primary colors that coursed over the building, on pipe railings in the large open foyer, in stairwells, on windows and door trim of offices and library, cafeteria and locker areas.

72

Kat took me into a home ec room—more warmth, more brightness. We sat down and began to talk. Her words spilled out, too fast for me to take good notes. I was grateful for the little tape recorder, and happy that it seemed to bother no one during many hours of interviewing at all three schools.

Empowerment: Teaching and Working Together

Kat's opening remark set the tone for the rest of the conversations we were to have: "One of the signs of empowerment is that *I can do this* (leadership) *right along with being in the classroom.*" For her, empowerment was not at all external to her teaching, but rather an integral part of it. The classroom was still the main arena. Confident about her own teaching, Kat relished joining her efforts with those of her colleagues. The willingness to team and to share, she thinks, is another sign of empowered teachers, and essential for a faculty attempting to reach a common vision:

> I've always felt the need to look closely at what my teaching is. But empowerment also comes from working with others in the department who will share and team. I like best finding interdisciplinary ways to solve issues, whether it's for the student or for the whole school. MIL has allowed us to ask ourselves, "What if we had our best wish come true?" We haven't always thought that way, but now we can. MIL gave us the feeling that we aren't as locked in. We are no longer saying that we have no control over things [although] there are some things that we still can't do much about. But the importance of what I—what we—say as teachers—that's growing. That's why we have a tremendous responsibility to watch what we say. We do have a power that we didn't. It's come from working together and finding more common purposes.

Practical about some of the tougher aspects of teaming and sharing, Kat noted that teachers haven't had time even for casual socializing, much less practice in talking about issues that are based in teaching values rarely expressed to each other:

73

> Most of us haven't been used to having our ways questioned. To be able to accept that there may be a different way that is better, that's another sign of empowerment. We are still learning to talk with each other about this. As we began to make our voices heard, it was hurtful at first. We aren't prepared for this. But we need to do it—to build a process so that we can say our minds in a kind way.

Think of the complexity, for instance, involved in a Steering Committee discussion that must include and address the problem of litter in the halls (one contingent's chief gripe) to tougher topics like scheduling time differently (everybody is vested in this) to more personal and sensitive issues like: "Some feel they're carrying the burden for all."

Kat's skills, even as she admits the need to hone them, are backed by her familiarity and acceptance of the little woes and large differences that bedevil any group of professionals working together in a new way. Credibility is bolstered by her obvious concern for the group's impact on the general good:

> We just kept on going, trying to keep in touch with monthly meetings, keeping the agenda open for all. When I feel worst is when we have too many focus points. That's when litter gets handled accordingly. It's not a put-down, but priorities become clear when we keep asking, "What's best for Norbridge?"

Leadership of this kind, able to balance faculty feelings and individual needs against a larger sense of school mission, is distinctly teacher-like.

How Teaching and Leading Affect Each Other

Kat has given plenty of thought to teaching and, increasingly, how teaching and leading affect one another. That classroom perspective enhances teacher leadership is clear to her: "The classroom keeps my focus, it gives credibility. They can say, 'She knows—she's there.'" Kat also offered a look at the flip side—at what leading does to teaching:

74

If teachers don't develop leadership skills, I don't believe they can do as well in the classroom. We're preparing our kids to question, give input and make choices. Don't we have to model that for them in the way we do our own work?

Kat saw her first responsibility to her students, yet she took very seriously her charge of elected leadership. In asking herself, "Was that hour just spent on leadership or is it related to one of my classes?" she often found the lines blurred; the answer can be both. Ordering and managing time for both roles are problems for Kat. "Focusing more and then building a framework" to increase faculty collaboration can lessen the double load of teaching and leadership, but the balancing act takes its toll: "You can wear out pretty fast." And if she can't do both well, Kat is positive about one thing: "If I have to go into administration to do what I want to do—I just won't."

Teacher Leadership and Administration

Although teachers may not articulate it as such, they have an instinctual feel for the difference between administration and leadership. Certain opinions expressed by Kat seem valuable for further exploration.

First, she sees that administrative training creates a certain aura that simply does not fit with a teacher culture:

It's almost like they have to wear a label that says, "I should know." And they begin to believe it. As a teacher there's a lot I know and a lot I don't know. I'm comfortable with that.

Next, Kat acknowledges that single biggest waste of the single biggest resource we have in education—teacher expertise and teacher wisdom:

There are also lots of things I'm good at. Aren't they missing a lot of expertise when one group of people spends so much time making decisions, without being tuned into kids and teachers? Why don't they come out here and interact? They

75

get so tied to specifics, like this or that "learner-based outcome." We could work together—I'd be willing to team with an administrator—on something like exploring with our students what it is to grow old in this community.

Leadership and Empowerment

Co-chairing the Steering Committee with Kat is Jim, a special ed teacher. It is his belief that teacher empowerment and leadership demand change in the way teachers—and he includes himself—work, not only with students but with each other. Jim's conversation, like Kat's, is sprinkled with "teaming" and "sharing." He focuses on the everlasting problem of teacher isolation, and the need to get teachers to work together to effect their own changes and to serve as models for their students: "How am I going to teach kids to work together on an assembly line if I persist in just doing my own thing?" Jim knows, too, the waste of talent that, with more conscious collaboration, teachers could "bottle and share."

Acknowledging that some colleagues find new view-points and new practices difficult, Jim traces this not to indifference—a charge often leveled at teachers—but to school structures that deny teachers the time they demand for careful experimentation with new ideas:

Sure, some of the faculty possibly have no desire for leadership, but I think at least half of the teachers are willing to take on a lot more responsibility, to share and to do their thing differently. But they must be met halfway in terms of time. And I don't think that's a cop-out.

Jim next notes an important distinction between teacher leadership and teacher empowerment. Leadership is inherent in the teaching role, embedded in teacher collegiality, as often tacit as expressed. However, many teacher leaders finally conclude that empowerment, or a sense of real efficacy, demands an enabling structure in which their leadership can be expressed.

The lack of positional power in teachers' leadership bothers Jim. Teachers' classroom autonomy fades outside those walls, and as for actual power to "make things move," he says:

> We don't have control over the essential things [like getting the time]. Our hands are still tied in terms of getting people to give us certain roles. [Authority] has to come from above—as though it is not going to mean as much if any one of us in the building said it. I have a hard time with that. Why should it mean anything more coming from the principal than from the home ec teacher or the art teacher?

Leadership, the Teacher Mission, and Time

The necessity of reducing or leaving entirely direct work with students to find time for leadership presents another problem for Jim. He returns to the issue of time and the conflict experienced by teachers who decided they had to move into administration to "get things done:"

> There has to be a different way to look at the time we have available. I think any . . . teacher who has moved into administration has felt this conflict: I am getting away from being with the students, [where] I can see the immediate effect and where I want to be. On the other hand, if I can get myself in a situation where I am the one making decisions, that can affect my students.

Throughout this study, the problem of time in the teaching day presented the greatest deterrent to general teacher interest in assuming new roles. It is not lack of desire or ability—as is presumed by many outside of teaching—but a genuine fear that the new role will be tacked on to their already exhausting schedule.

Collegial Checks and Balances

Jim saw collegial response and reaction as critical to teacher leaders' success, mentioning an informal but powerful check and balance that faculty teams exercise to keep their

77

leadership on target. Leaders who are answerable only to someone on an organizational chart are one thing. But leadership that comes from the group is different. He didn't worry about "straying," he said, from team or faculty goals:

> Your colleagues won't let you. That's the thing that I think will work . . . . Your colleagues will let you know one way or another that you're getting too far off the stream of what the team wants you to do.

Appleton

I had to fly to the coast and then back several hundred miles to travel to Martin. The little town was not only literally remote, but its rich, rolling hills along the river emanated an air of other-worldliness. It was easy to find Appleton Elementary School. Well-named, it lies above Martin in an area of fruit orchards. Sheep with their lambs grazed in a small yard only a stone's throw from the school's playground.

No students or teachers appeared to have arrived yet, but the principal met me at the door. We went to the faculty lounge for a cup of coffee; a huge urn had already finished perking, ready for incoming faculty and staff. I soon left to find the MIL Steering Committee Chair.

Gayle was alone in her classroom, already at work (it was not yet 7:30) arranging displays for the day's lessons. This picture remains with me, made all the more vivid by a remark that exemplifies her energy in combining leadership with the joy and the rigors of teaching:

> I do my best job every day and I don't have any days I don't like. I don't have any days that I don't want to come to work.

Our interviews were sprinkled with the word "confidence." If anything informed Gayle's sense of empowerment and teacher leadership, it was a sense of confidence—in the effects of leadership on her teaching and in the special quality that her continuing teaching gave her leadership. She credits the teacher association with developing this confidence:

> It made a difference in my entire life—I learned leadership through the Association and, in fact, I became a better teacher because of that. They gave me confidence, and a lot of it came from information. You cannot be confident about yourself and your ability if you don't have information.

The State of Teachers and Teaching

Gayle believes in her colleagues, veterans and new teachers alike, stating that "society should be grateful for the strength and quality" of those who have come and are still coming—for whatever reason—into the profession. Nevertheless, she admits that typical school governance structures have encouraged "stagnant and blase" attitudes in some teachers, keeping them uninformed and thus seemingly uninterested in change—"before this program most teachers didn't understand there was a reform movement going." Another reason she gives for this condition is the gender factor—the profession's high composition of women—that is especially powerful in elementary schools:

> It's right and proper and easier [for many teachers] to be directed what to do—"I really don't have time for that. I have to teach school. I don't want to figure out how to schedule the lunch room. Tell me what to do and I am going to do it."

Even so, the number of women teachers with this traditional attitude is diminishing. Younger women teachers, Gayle says, come from a newer, different culture that sees direction from a single source of authority as neither necessary nor helpful. Drawing a parallel between democratic classrooms and democratic schools, Gayle explains that, just as children are no longer responding well to autocratic teachers, so teachers can no longer work effectively with autocratic administrators:

79

Teachers . . . no longer accept being led autocratically. The whole idea of shared decision making has to come down to better teaching—and better learners.

Leadership Development for Teachers

If teachers do need leadership roles to make schools more democratic as well as to "learn their potential," Gayle makes a strong case for more formal leadership development for teachers. She includes the need for such practical training as skills in interpersonal relations and communication:

The first thing we did was to have a communications skills workshop. When we did our survey, that was one of the things we needed. Even though we thought we were a good working faculty, we did lack that.

Gayle stressed that learning to relate with the public and developing community and corporate consensus about the mission of schooling is also necessary for teacher leaders, whose typical education does not include study of organization development, public/governmental relations, or adult learning:

When I went into education, I thought education led society. I think we need to take a leadership role, we need to describe the problem, and give the public our idea of what could be. The description should come from us; it is our job as educators to educate them. If we told everyone the story, they would be with us. Everybody wants the same thing—the very best for the children of this country. We are just fighting about how to get there. We have all failed on that.

Teacher Leaders and Administration

Many teacher leaders share a sentiment Gayle expressed about the lack of desire they feel for an administrative career. And yet, to "make things happen," with direct impact on teaching and learning, some practitioners have reluctantly left teaching—a profound choice, with profound implications. Leadership loses those teachers who will not leave; the students lose those who feel

80

they must. Gayle would not leave and is firm about the need for new kinds of leadership development:

> I once thought about being an administrator. I took one administration class. I never would be an administrator. The kind of information and skills I'm talking about [for teacher leadership] is not for becoming anything; it clearly is for career teachers.

Time and Leadership

All teacher leadership talk eventually devolves to the topic of time, and Gayle is no exception. She disputes the widely held perception that teachers are not "committed" simply because they do not find time for tasks and responsibilities that are added on to a full teaching load:

> There is high commitment among teachers for their own leadership and each other's, but there are only so many hours in the day. They have to change the amount of time we're spending in the classroom. I think we could find real correlation between giving teachers the time to become informed, to improve their workplace, to develop leadership skills, and every child in their classrooms benefitting.

Another knot in this problem is that time for leadership often equals time away from the classroom; teacher leaders take a lot of criticism from principals, fellow teachers and parents over "missing school." Her concern has a personal side to it, but she is clear about the necessity of viewing time differently:

> I have taken some flack for it [leaving the classroom for committee work and attendance at conferences], but I feel real firm about it. I feel that in myself, I can justify it. The quantity of time doesn't insure quality, anyway. You know yourself that out of a 55-minute period you don't always get 55 minutes of quality. To have done what we did here in this project would have taken years . . . we may never have done it. But because we were given the time to sit down within the

81

day and plan together, we have proved without a shadow of doubt what teachers could do.

Teacher Empowerment and Principal Empowerment

What did the teachers at Appleton accomplish because of teacher leadership of the MIL project? An important change was the formation of the school's committee structure. The faculty designed four committees—teacher-to-student, teacher-to-teacher, teacher-to-administrator and teacher-to-community. The committees facilitated a decision-making process that covered a broad, school-wide spectrum of needs. One committee's product was a teacher-written document spelling out agreed-upon areas for faculty involvement.

Another innovation, "teacher-convened" faculty meetings offered insights regarding Gayle's style of leadership and its reflection in the way the teachers developed their own styles. Some teachers were uncomfortable about convening (leading) faculty meetings, "but we have all practiced and we have all done it." One refreshing comment alluded to the collegial informality of the four committees: "We have [committee chairs], but we don't use them much."

A significant outcome of the project at Appleton was the principal's willingness to risk changes in his role that stemmed from the empowerment of teachers' roles. He admitted that it wasn't easy explaining to fellow principals that he hadn't given away his authority—or as he put it, "the keys to the building." On occasion, he had had to say, "I am sorry, but I cannot live with what you are suggesting, and we cannot do that."

A mutual trust and cooperation prevailed. The principal did admit that he had been surprised and even made somewhat uncomfortable by certain aspects of the teacher-initiated committee structure; for instance, the teacher-to-administrator committee came up with guidelines for principal evaluation, and he actually found it a positive experience. Some of the deepest feelings I encountered in this study came out in this principal's final interview. He volunteered that, as a result of this teacher-led project, he himself "had never felt more empowered"— his own work was better and it was simply easier to get things done. He allowed me to share that remark with Gayle. Her reply was both matter-of-fact and right at the heart of the matter:

> If he had asked us to do some of these things, we would never have done them. But now, deciding ourselves what we want to do, we do it ourselves. Just ask the people in the trenches and they will tell you how to restructure . . .

DIFFERENT VIEWS AND COMMON THEMES

On one hand, teacher leaders thought about and talked about empowerment and leadership in quite different ways. According to Nathan (Woodson) empowerment was the ability to make decisions about curriculum and other matters close to his work with students. Kat (Norbridge) saw her leadership as empowered by "working with others who will share and team." Jim (Norbridge) looked at teachers' lack of empowerment in that their "hands were tied" in gaining certain roles. Gayle (Appleton) said she "learned" leadership and confidence through working with the teacher association, stressing the importance of "information."

Four common themes emerged from the interviews and observations:

- Teaching mission and leadership effects upon one another

- Teacher leadership and collegial relationships

- Differences between teacher leadership and administration

- Time and teacher leadership

Effect of Teaching Mission
and Leadership Upon One Another

Nathan felt that Julia's leadership lacked credibility because she was no longer teaching. Only teachers, he thought, can understand the kind of leadership that other teachers believe necessary for real impact on teaching and learning. Kat saw her teaching enhanced by her leadership role, and her leadership strengthened among her colleagues because of her active classroom role. Jim was interested in leading teachers to share their thoughts about teaching in ways that will actually change the way schools work. Gayle knew that an essential for leading restructured schools was the ability to understand and respect teaching and teachers. She clearly felt good about her colleagues and her profession, about being a teacher.

These teacher leaders found an instinctive fit between teaching and leading. Foreign as this combination may be to education, these teacher leaders have nevertheless chosen to embark upon an uncharted course in a belief that their new roles might address the needs of students, schools, and their profession.

Teacher Leadership and Collegial Relations

Nathan believed that the abilities to sense faculty-wide needs, build consensus, and articulate visions that teachers find valid are qualities best found in leaders whose primary role is classroom teaching. Beth began her new leadership with an appreciation of career teachers, their viewpoints and their value—thus reaffirming her own teaching role. Kat expressed concern for the hurt that Norbridge teachers felt when they first began to speak their minds and question each other about deeply held beliefs. Jim sympathized with teachers who suffered the image of indifference when, in fact, their interest in leadership was overwhelmed by the demands of an unrealistic school schedule. Gayle's leadership acknowledged and accepted teacher differences through a committee structure that allowed teachers to participate in school change according to their skills and interests.

It is true that non-teaching leaders forget quickly what they once understood; it may even be true that non-teaching leaders never really valued teaching nor its practitioners. But successful teacher leaders, by definition, remain teachers with high regard for their colleagues and the unique perspective they share by virtue of their work with students.

Differences Between Teacher Leadership and Administration

Julia's vision of leadership was based more on managerial and controlling aspects of power than on influence acquired through shared understandings and collegial respect. Her replacement, Beth, was keenly aware of the negative connotations teachers attached to administrative control; she appreciated teachers' preference for determining their own needs. Kat found that administrative training and leadership styles did not fit with teacher beliefs, and that leadership roles which took teachers out of teaching were neither desirable nor in touch with what really happens in schools. Jim spoke of the conflict forced on teachers who felt they had to leave the classroom for the authority and power of administrative positions. Gayle flatly stated, "I would never be an administrator," and saw the need for a development program specifically for teachers that prepared them for new kinds of leadership roles allowing them to retain their mission as classroom teachers.

The old argument—whether one must leave teaching for leadership roles—is based on a choice that may not have to be made much longer. Teachers may soon be able to make decisions affecting their students and also stay with those students in schools with newly organized structures that empower teachers to assume leadership roles.

Nathan wanted leadership that will address the mechanistic way teacher time is used with "everybody plugged into a slot every period of the day" and that will find teachers the time to develop the curriculum that they are responsible for teaching. Kat mentioned the tensions of managing and balancing time between teaching and leadership tasks. Jim said there has to be a "different way to look at time," calling it an "essential" that teachers had no ability to control. Gayle was convinced of the need for a restructured school day that would allow teacher leaders appropriate time for both teaching and leadership.

The question of time remains the most complex. In one sense, the entire structure of school has emerged from ideas of time and work. Teachers, by changing and expanding their own work to include new leadership roles, may offer one key to the puzzle once they have the freedom to use time in ways that have yet to be envisioned.

CONCLUSIONS AND RECOMMENDATIONS

Even with different views and working in different contexts, teacher leaders have been thinking common thoughts and expressing common concerns about school leadership in general, and their own leadership roles, in particular.

Although they may not be conversant with the body of literature on empowerment, leadership, and restructuring, teachers and especially teacher leaders could have written much of it. They affirm the reform writers at every turn. They recognize with painful clarity that they are powerless, lacking the status, knowledge, and access to decision making that are Maeroff's (1988a) indicators of empowerment. They know better than anyone the numbing effects of bureaucracy (Frymier 1987) on genuine efforts to restructure curriculum and policy in authentic ways. They are wholeheartedly in agreement with Devaney (1987), Lieberman (1988), and Little (1988) in sticking to their

86

guns about a new vision of leadership that scorns hierarchy and "promotion" and values their sense of collegiality and professionalism. They believe the need for their leadership is great enough and their credibility as leaders is strong enough to allow them to admit that, even though they have a lot to learn about leadership, they know what it must not be. They know their power is derived from their reasons for seeking leadership—concerns about teaching and learning (Johnston and Germinario 1986).

Enabling the Voice:
Exploration, Development, and Support

Eager to share their views, test their ideas, and discuss their desire for fresh knowledge and skills in this new area of leadership, these teachers seemed starved for opportunities to talk about their profession, their ideas, and their students. Besides the constant pressure of time, there is simply so much to say that is so hard to express, to explain. Even so, it seems preposterous that there are so few opportunities for deep and continuing dialogue between people vital to each other—and to the students they teach. It seems a legitimate need: a means for further development of their leadership and an audience for their views.

There are not presently widespread resources for facilitating this kind of dialogue or for offering the kind of information, training, and development that teacher leaders say they need: opportunities for study, reflection, and collegial exchange regarding the new roles and responsibilities they are increasingly assuming in addition to their classroom work. As school restructuring becomes more than a theoretical response to our nation's educational problems, the call may become clearer for exploration, development, and support of the role of teacher leadership and for a revaluing of its practitioners:

Once teachers "try on" leadership, they find that it fits them like a glove. As teachers become leaders, they come to view themselves as serious theoreticians as well as capable practitioners, as contributors to a collaborative process as well as individuals in classrooms, and as major decision makers in the educational process as well as implementors of programs. They come to value themselves and . . . each other; and in so doing, they transform the professional culture in which they work (Miller 1988, p. 172).

Recommendations[3]

The study of teacher leadership should be increased and should directly involve teacher leaders themselves. Common themes expressed by emerging teacher leaders need to be shared and tested with other school leaders, especially interested principals. Thus conscious constructions of a new paradigm for leadership in schools can be built and shared with practitioners across the nation to adapt to their own situations and their own students.

A formal effort must be made to design professional development programs for practicing and aspiring teacher leaders, based on their needs and the needs of faculties in schools attempting to restructure the ways they are organized and governed for teaching and learning.

FOOTNOTES

1. The research reported in this chapter was partially supported by the Instruction and Professional Development Unit of the National Education Association and by the NEA Mastery In Learning Project. It was originally presented as a paper at the American Educational Research Association annual meeting, Boston, MA, April 16, 1990.

2. Pseudonyms are used for participants and sites.

3. These recommendations are under consideration by an Indiana University team of teachers and professors who have received a Lilly Endowment planning grant for developing a Leadership Institute for the Future of Teaching (LIFT).

REFERENCES

Alutto, J. A., and Belasco, A. 1972. A typology for participation in organizational decision making. *Administrative Science Quarterly* 17:117–25.

Barth, R. S. 1990. *Improving schools from within.* San Francisco: Jossey Bass.

Barth, R. S. 1988. Principals, teachers and school leadership. *Phi Delta Kappan* 69: 639–42.

Boyer, E. L. 1988. The time has come—School reform: Completing the course. *NASSP Bulletin* 72(504): 61–68.

Brandt, R. 1989. On teacher empowerment: A conversation with Ann Lieberman. *Educational Leadership* 46(8): 23–26.

Cuban, L. 1988. A fundamental puzzle of school reform. *Phi Delta Kappan* 69: 341–344.

Devaney, K. 1987. *The lead teacher: Ways to begin.* New York: Carnegie Forum on Education and the Economy.

Erlandson, D. A., and S. L. Bifano. 1987. Teacher empowerment: What research says to the principal. *NASSP Bulletin* 71(503): 31–36.

Fay, C. 1989. *Teacher Leadership.* Unpublished manuscript. Indiana University, Bloomington.

Frymier, J. 1987. Bureaucracy and the neutering of teachers. *Phi Delta Kappan* 69:9–16.

Johnston, G. S., and Germinario, V. 1986. Relationship between teacher decisional status and loyalty. *Journal of Educational Administration* 23:91–105.

Lieberman, A. 1988. Teachers and principals: Turf, tension, and new tricks. *Phi Delta Kappan* 69:648–653.

Little, J. W. 1988. Assessing the prospects for teacher leadership. In *Building a professional culture in schools,* ed. A. Lieberman, 78–106. New York: Teachers College Press.

Maeroff, G. 1988a. A blueprint for empowering teachers. *Phi Delta Kappan* 69:472–77.

———. 1988b. The empowerment of teachers. *Phi Delta Kappan* 69: 472–77.

Miller, L. 1988. Unlikely beginnings: The district office as a starting point for developing a professional culture for teaching. In *Building a professional culture in schools,* ed. A. Lieberman, 167–85. New York: Teachers College Press.

Pratte, R., and Rury, J. L. 1988. Professionalism, autonomy, and teachers. *Educational Policy* 2:71–87.

Rice, K. 1987. *Empowering teachers: A search for professional autonomy.* Unpublished thesis, Dominican College of San Rafael, California (ERIC Document Reproduction Service No. ED 282 845).

Chapter 3

BECOMING A CHANGE FACILITATOR: THE FIRST-YEAR EXPERIENCE OF FIVE TEACHER LEADERS

by Ann Kilcher

School improvement through shared decision making requires new leadership roles for teachers. One formal role is change facilitator. Sara was one of five teachers who participated in a study of learning to be a change facilitator. Her case illustrates that teachers who become change facilitators require new knowledge, skills, and understandings. Their effectiveness is influenced by the strategies they employ to learn their role, their personal change facilitator style, and contextual factors that influence their learning and work. Districts can enhance change efforts through careful selection, training, and assignment of change facilitators.

The restructuring movement and the increased interest in site-based management and shared decision making is providing another avenue for teachers to exercise leadership. Changing schools requires the energy and skills of many people; in particular, it calls for teachers to actively participate in the action. One formal teacher leadership role is that of change facilitator. This chapter describes the first year experience of five teachers who provided leadership as change facilitators in a school improvement project in eastern Canada.

Project Improvement

Project Improvement was an initiative to introduce and implement school-based planning and management in the district. The Eastern School Board adopted a developmental strategy to move decision making and staff development to the school level. Five schools were selected to participate in the Project during its first year (1988–89). The immediate goal was to increase school level capacity for problem-solving, decision-making, communication, and planning. The focus for particular improvement projects was to be determined by individual staffs based on the unique situations and problems at each school.

A cadre of change facilitators was selected and trained to provide a support system for Project Improvement. The team of 13 facilitators was made up of classroom teachers, administrators, counselors, and consultants. Finally, each school selected a school leadership team, comprised of the principal and several teachers, to coordinate and facilitate improvement efforts at their respective schools. The change facilitators worked with school leadership teams and staffs, assisting, facilitating, and guiding them as they learned a problem-solving approach to school improvement. The facilitators were assigned in teams of two or three to work with one of the five schools in the Project.

The Study

This chapter is based upon a year-long study[1] conducted during the first year of Project Improvement (Kilcher 1991). The purpose of the study was to explore the processes associated with learning to be a change facilitator. The investigation also addressed questions about style and the influence of context on the learning and work of change facilitators during their first year in the role.

The investigation employed a multi-case study design. The five participants were selected to represent different placement settings and contrasting personal characteristics. Data were collected six times during the 1988–89 school year at regular intervals from participants, project coordinators, district administrators, and school personnel. The primary source of data was interview transcripts which were supplemented by journal entries and documents. Following data analysis, individual case descriptions were written for each participant. A cross-case analysis revealed themes, patterns, and contrasts in the process of learning to be a change facilitator; these, in turn, influenced the formulation of recommendations.

THE CASE OF SARA NICKERSON

Sara was starting her fifth year as a teacher in the district's Gifted Program; a pull-out program for approximately 250 fifth through eighth grade students in the school district. As a teacher of the gifted, she also conducted workshops and provided consultation to other teachers on enrichment learning experiences for students. Sara had eleven years of teaching experience during which she had taught all grade levels and many subjects. She was also in the process of completing a masters degree with a speciality in the education of the gifted and talented. Sara was 43, married, and the mother of two teenage boys.

Initial Impressions

Sara explained her concept of facilitator at the beginning:

A facilitator means catalyst in the background . . . somebody who helps the process move. . . . I don't see myself as an instructor . . . but as an agent who gets to know people well enough to help them come to their own decisions . . . a person who helps them learn to work together, build as a unit, and begin to know each other better, take risks and start to take more responsibility for what goes on in their own schools.

She was very interested in the Project and identified some specific learning goals:

To me, the bottom line is going to be what teachers get out of it, because . . . that's where change is going to happen, in the classroom. So I definitely expect to and want to learn about effective teaching strategies—what works and what the research is telling us. Also, change stuff . . . human consciousness.

Sara also expressed some concerns. "My main concern is about how much time it will take . . . about spreading myself too thin . . . and the unknown, the *what if* situations." In general, however, she was looking forward to the year ahead, anticipating that it would "be very exciting."

St. Joseph's School

Sara was assigned to St. Joseph's School, a small K–12 school in a lower socioeconomic area of the city. Many of the students came from disadvantaged backgrounds and there was a high dropout rate. The administration was described as "very open," but the principal was seen as "indecisive" and as a "fence sitter."

St. Joseph's was described as a "family kind of school." Sara remarked, "There's a community kind of feeling." The staff were perceived as risk-takers. One of the coordinators commented, "The climate is one of calm and laughter and support." He continued, "With the exception of a few teachers, you see more positive interactions going on between staff and students and teachers than you will in most schools."

The staff was considered ready for change. The superintendent explained, "They see themselves as already doing a lot of what this involves. They have been trying to improve their school over the last number of years on more of a helter skelter basis . . . and they have slowly started to turn around the image of the school." In the spring of 1988, the staff at St. Joseph's participated in a workshop day where they began to assess the strengths and weaknesses of the school. Subsequently, the administrators chose three priorities, and committees were

94

formed and were in place when the school entered Project Improvement.

Sara's Activities, Events, Learnings, and Concerns

The first year as a change facilitator was a busy one for Sara. Not only did she participate actively in events and meetings at St. Joseph's, she was also involved in district-level activities, conducted workshops at other schools, and participated in a provincial leadership conference.

Jumping In: The Fall Term

Sara took a proactive stance and became involved immediately with the school. She and her partner initiated a visit to St. Joseph's School during the first week of classes. A twenty minute discussion with the principal and vice-principal resulted in decisions to have a leadership team meeting, a staff meeting, and a full-day professional development session by mid-October.

Sara was caught off guard after the first leadership team meeting when two of the members asked for written feedback about the meeting. This led Sara to inquire about coaching, giving feedback, and the debriefing process. She discussed the request for feedback with Project coordinators and other core facilitators at their meeting that same evening. In her journal entry that night she wrote, "I realized that we should have built in time at the end of the meeting to discuss their views on how it went." She also made notes on guidelines for facilitating at meetings:

- If no one else is leading, take the initiative.

- Ask leading questions.

- Bring the group back on task.

- Build in time at the end of the meeting to ask them how they felt the meeting went/give feedback.

- Before you adjourn, nail down the date of the next meeting, and ask who will volunteer to facilitate/lead the next meeting and be responsible for the agenda.

During the third week of September, Sara facilitated an exercise to establish belief statements at a staff meeting, attended a steering committee meeting, and had a long conversation with another facilitator about confidentiality and the role they were learning. That week's journal entry illustrates Sara's thinking on the process and her role as change facilitator:

> How much does the change facilitator observe and just serve as resource person, and how much intervention/directed guidance is necessary? If we do intervene, are we saying the school improvement process is a recipe, and they aren't following the formula? Would that criticism circumvent or damage the team at this trust-building stage? Wheels-within-wheels . . . what a complicated, convoluted dynamic is human interaction!

During the next two weeks, Sara attended two leadership team meetings to debrief the staff meeting and to plan for the full-day inservice session in October. The second week of October proved to be busy with three major events: a change facilitator meeting, a full-day inservice session at St. Joseph's, and our second research interview. At the change facilitator meeting, Sara found the "clarification about the school profile and the discussion on evaluation very helpful." St. Joseph's inservice day was devoted to awareness presentations and discussions on change, school improvement research, and the superintendent's vision. Her role was participant-observer, and she found this role somewhat frustrating.

> It was a good day . . . but if I had the responsibility of planning the day myself, I probably would have done some things differently. Then, at least I would have felt that it was my fault

96

. . . the success or failure was due to me. But this way, in the facilitating role, it's an unsatisfactory feeling in a sense.

Figuring out the school improvement process and the change facilitator role were major themes in the fall.

It's not any easier than I expected it would be . . . sometimes it's really . . . tiresome [laughter]. . . . all this process stuff can really wear you down. . . . Process is really, in many ways, it is the end. It's not the final product that is most important, the process is the product.

She expressed confusion and uncertainty about her facilitator role.

I still have doubts about my own effectiveness in the role of facilitator. I think I am a good group member, but not sure that I have the necessary skill to remain aloof from the process, while retaining just the right touch of involvement to spur things along, or to bring them back on task, or to see that everyone is participating. It's hard work to do this well, this constant monitoring of the process without being obvious or controlling the group.

In speaking about the roles she was playing Sara stated, "I'm a facilitator, a learner, a coach, just a friend, maybe advisor sometimes, sounding board, affirmer, listener." Sara also found herself being an ambassador for the project. She identified some skills and strategies she was using in her facilitating role such as 1-3-6 (a group decision-making strategy), brainstorming, coaching and debriefing. Interestingly, she also reported using these strategies with kids and in her work with colleagues.

Sara continued to attend meetings for the remainder of the fall: three leadership team meetings and a parent meeting at St. Joseph's, two steering committee meetings, and another facilitator meeting. For the most part, her role was participant-observer and resource person, since the leadership team assumed responsibility for facilitating meetings at the school. She would sit quietly and listen intently, interjecting her opinions when asked or when she had a contribution to make.

At a leadership team meeting in November, Sara found herself in conflict over the issue of student involvement in the process. Sara verbalized her hypothesis that Project Improvement was ultimately concerned with staff development for teachers. At that point, one of the staff members "brought up his frustration that this whole Project was student-centered and had not yet involved students. . . . He suggested that one of them might sit in on the leadership meetings." Sara and the teacher argued their respective positions until the other change facilitator brought the meeting back to order. The incident had an impact on Sara. "It caused me to do some introspection. . . . I'm not really very good with confrontation, and I know that about myself."

The fall term ended on a busy note with four activities in a ten-day span just before Christmas. Again, Sara's primary role was that of participant-observer. At the change facilitator meeting, she participated in a reflection activity on the role, and offered her suggestions on a networking day that was being planned for January. The steering committee spent a full day considering strategic planning for the district to establish a vision and goals for the next decade.

Role clarification was an issue throughout the fall. In November Sara declared, "I'm still not really sure what a core facilitator is supposed to do . . . sometimes I feel like they don't really need us." She expressed concerns about time, focus, isolation, and diversion.

Sara identified time as a concern in the initial interview and brought it up repeatedly in our discussions. Another concern related to time was focus. Sara had eclectic interests and a need to seek out information. She found herself pulled in divergent directions.

I'm all over the place . . . because of my master's program in Connecticut, I'm still trying to read and do things for that . . . because of my school work, I'm mired in the area of enrichment . . . and then I'm looking for things about drama, because I'm teaching creative drama with kids . . . and then I'm looking for stuff on school improvement and change . . . and then because I'm interested, I occasionally find articles on thinking skills or creativity . . . I'm reading all over the place. I would like to be able to zero in and focus more on the role, but there are so many other things that I'm responsible for.

Isolation and diversion also impacted Sara. She found herself working in isolation because her teammate, Rob, assigned to co-facilitate at St. Joseph's, did not have as much time as he anticipated. Other responsibilities diverted Sara's attention and energy. By the end of November she was feeling overwhelmed to the point that we discussed the possibility of her withdrawing either from the study or from the change facilitator role altogether.

A Busy Time: The Winter Term

The winter term continued to be hectic for Sara with meetings and five professional development days. She spent less time at St. Joseph's and more time on district-level improvement activities. The first event after Christmas was a networking day for the leadership teams from the schools, the change facilitators, and the steering committee members. It was a day of sharing and professional development sessions for the five schools involved in the Project. Sara was very enthusiastic about the day, and she thought it went exceptionally well. "It was a real morale booster for everybody. . . . There was a kind of coming together . . . a synergy."

During the last two weeks of January, she attended a steering committee meeting, a change facilitator meeting, and a leadership team meeting. The major item on the steering committee agenda was review and critique of a readiness package that had been developed by a subcommittee to introduce new schools to the school improvement process. Change was the professional development topic at the facilitator meeting where findings from two recent change studies were presented and discussed. The purpose of the leadership team meeting was planning for the February inservice day.

At the end of January, Sara talked about her changing understanding of the facilitator role:

> In the fall . . . I thought you've got to be at all these meetings, and you've got [snaps fingers] to, to help these people . . . and now I'm relaxing a little bit, and I think the change facilitator's role is far more one of support. Be a good listener. Make suggestions when they are appropriate or when you see something that might help one of them with something that they're struggling with. It's their school . . . you have to let people make their own decisions, even if they are not the decisions you would have made.

When discussing key learnings at the half way point of the year, Sara responded, "When I think about key learnings, I almost invariably will relate it to something read—when I see something in print . . . it's assimilated better for me." She highlighted learning about stages in team process and team development, the Concerns Based Adoption Model, presentation styles, and working with groups. Again, she mentioned the conflict in November. "I really do dislike conflict and I sometimes avoid or accommodate. I guess I'm more accommodating than avoiding." At the conclusion of the January interview Sara stated, "I'm happy to be doing what I'm doing, despite all the difficulties of the last couple of months. I don't want to withdraw from either the study or the Project."

February was full of activity with three inservice days and a series of meetings. Sara was asked to conduct a session on developing a vision and mission statement at the St. Joseph's inservice day. The following week, she facilitated a small group exercise on developing a school vision at a provincial leadership conference. She also served as a resource person by providing a the session leader with articles and suggestions. At the end of the session Sara was approached by a principal from another district about the possibility of facilitating a day with her staff in May.

Sara also attended an "excellent" change facilitator meeting where they engaged in a "powerful" teambuilding exercise and discussed the possibility of reorganizing change facilitator assignments so there would be an internal/external team of people working together in each school the following year. In addition, they reviewed the resources that the Project coordinators were collecting. Later, at a leadership team meeting at St. Joseph's, they discussed dealing with resistance and blocking from some staff members.

Sara had the opportunity to practice the new skills and strategies she was learning during the Gifted Program workshop and inservice day. Sara assumed the role of facilitator when her own staff at the Gifted Center spent a day "looking at themselves and their program, and writing a mission statement." In her weekly reflection she commented, "There's no doubt that the strategies and information we've gained as core facilitators have influenced and helped us in our roles at the Gifted Center."

Sara had volunteered to be part of a working group on a revision of the readiness package that had been presented in January. Just prior to spring break, two meetings of a readiness working group were held to agree on the organization and format of the document and how they would proceed.

In March, Sara spoke about the range of roles she was playing: "committee member, organizer, researcher, presenter, planner, and morale booster." She discussed the influence of her own learning on her students and, in particular, commended the effectiveness of the decision making strategies. Sara wished she had more time for the Project and reported that she "continued to read all over the place because of [her] interest in everything." For her, time, focus, momentum and continuation were concerns.

Accelerating to the End: The Spring Term

The spring term became busier, and activity accelerated rather than slowing down for the year as Sara had anticipated. Meetings continued to be the dominant event. District level meetings and activities as well as a school-based workshop in another district consumed Sara's energy and attention in the third portion of the first year.

Sara worked intensively on the readiness package with another steering committee member during the first ten days of April. They compiled a set of articles, discussion guides, and exercises for staffs to begin exploring school-based improvement and staff development.

The leadership team met to plan for the rest of the year. The change facilitators met to discuss the first year evaluation, the facilitator retreat in June, and suggestions for the summer training institute. In addition, she attended leadership team meetings at St. Joseph's to plan for the May workshop day on self-esteem.

Preparing for and leading a professional development day for a school in another district provided Sara with a focus to think about the various activities involved in the process and sort out what was important in order to help a new school staff get started. This was a very significant learning event for her. Five full pages of her journal were devoted to her thoughts and reflections on this workshop.

Sara also learned about self-concept through her involvement at St. Joseph's workshop day. She was very impressed with the day in general, but specifically with a "parent who was quite vocal and inspiring." Sara ended her journal entry on this event with a maxim: "An outstanding feature of mentally healthy individuals is that they are able to RISK."

June was a month of summarizing and evaluating year one of Project Improvement and planning for year two. All of the groups in which Sara had participated were taking stock of the year and evaluating progress. At the year-end facilitators' retreat, Sara used the analogy of a teacher on a wilderness camping trip to describe her year. "It had its thrilling moments, lows too . . . . We didn't know what we were doing . . . but people expected that we knew the way out." A highlight for Sara during the year was observing all the personal and professional growth in others.

Sara had been invited to help with the summer training of the new school leadership teams. The training team met an evening and two full days to plan the August leadership institute. Sara found "the experience of helping plan this training tremendously beneficial . . . it forces you to reexamine the whole idea of school improvement, and to analyze what people need to know, and how to help them."

The steering committee held their final dinner meeting on June 14th. Sara met with the principal from St. Mary's school to debrief from the May workshop and attended a meeting to finish the readiness package. She also dropped in at St. Joseph's and needed to "remind them of finishing their tasks" before the end of the year. Finally, Sara facilitated a review of the year with the leadership team.

In summary, Sara spent many hours and days in her new role as change facilitator. She spent approximately 15 professional days in her various roles and nearly 28 additional days in meetings, events, activities, and interviews. The rest of the learning and work was done during personal time.

Sara ended her year with some firm thoughts on the role of a change facilitator:

Facilitating . . . is like trying to do inquiry teaching. It means leading people to discover things for themselves . . . and even though you may think that you have some answers, they don't mean anything to people unless they come from inside, or unless . . . they connect with something other people are thinking.

One of the coordinators summarized Sara's effective style:

She builds credibility in a relatively short period of time. I think a lot of it's her personality . . . the group will turn to her and I think that's where she's building the credibility. When the group turns to her she has her observations to make and she has a sense of giving them direction, as well, because she can give direction when she's turned to. . . . She has a perception that she is an outsider and that she's going to lay back and not be overly directive with the group . . . she's not going to be jumping in and trying to grab control.

SUMMARIZING THE FIRST YEAR
FOR TEACHERS AS CHANGE FACILITATORS

The first year in any new role is normally a time of excitement, anxiety, and intense learning. This was the case for the five teachers serving as change facilitators. The teachers gained new knowledge and skills and used a number of strategies to learn about facilitating change. The individuals had a range of facilitating styles and were influenced by different factors and people during the year.

New Knowledge, Skills, and Understandings

All the facilitators increased their understandings about change and the school improvement process. During the year they learned about school profiles, mission statements, goal setting, workplace cultures, monitoring and evaluation, planning, and adult learning. As the year progressed, their understanding of the complexity of the change process grew, and they realized how much more there was to learn.

The facilitators learned new strategies for working with groups of people, guiding problem solving and decision-making, conducting effective meetings, and coaching. The teachers also refined their interpersonal skills. They identified increased understanding of human behavior, group dynamics, conflict resolution, and teamwork as important learnings.

Perhaps the most trying challenge for the teacher-facilitators in their first year was figuring out what they were supposed to be doing. Learning to be a change facilitator was a process of role clarification and negotiation. Despite training, and the ongoing support of a team of others learning the same role, each individual was faced with negotiating his or her role in a particular context.

Each of the facilitators learned about themselves. The very nature of the role and the improvement process required each to examine his or her own strengths and weaknesses, attitudes and behaviors, and the impact of those behaviors on others.

Multiple Learning Strategies

All of the teachers employed multiple strategies to learn about facilitating change. At times, each chose to learn alone and, at other times, to learn with others.

Learning Alone

Reflection was identified by each of the participants as a key learning strategy. Everyone commented on the journal writing and how it helped them to reflect and articulate their thinking. Involvement in the research study also forced each participant to examine his or her learning in a systematic way. *Reading* was another solitary learning strategy used by all facilitators. It was a primary strategy for Sara and a secondary strategy for the other four. *Organizing* was a form of individual learning unique to one individual. He spent hours reviewing, researching, and reorganizing materials on his own. He learned as he sifted and sorted and prepared packages to take to a meeting or professional development day.

Learning with Others

Discussions and meetings with others were important to the learning process for everyone. Other facilitators and the Project coordinators provided support, encouragement, and different perspectives. Three of the five facilitators learned from *being actively involved* and found it a challenge to take on a task, serve on a committee, or assume responsibility to provide leadership for a group. Observation was a primary learning strategy for one teacher and a supplementary process for the

105

others. All five stressed the importance of *training* and advocated organized and structured learning events with others to get started. They also emphasized the need for ongoing formal opportunities to continue learning.

Orientation, Perspective, Opportunities, and Concerns

Orientation, perspective, opportunities, and concerns affected each facilitator learning during the first year. The individual's orientation—*learning versus leading*—influenced both the learning experience and their facilitating approach. Facilitators who saw themselves as co-learners seemed to have a less frustrating experience and ran into less resistance when they provided guidance and direction than those who saw their role in terms of providing directive leadership.

Some of the facilitators played roles in more than one Project school. Individuals who were facilitators in other schools and clients in their own schools had the advantage of being able to compare and contrast *insider and outsider* perspectives. Being an outside facilitator seemed to be much more difficult than participating as an staff member in the school improvement process. Outside facilitators struggled with finding ways to remove themselves from the substance of the reform agenda at their client schools and concentrate instead on the processes of school improvement and change. The insiders, on the other hand, had opportunities to contribute their substantive ideas, as well as facilitate change in their own schools.

Opportunities dictated the roles and functions that different individuals assumed. All facilitators were involved to some degree in acting as a resource person, presenting, facilitating small groups, planning, organizing, and serving as committee members. Activities of two facilitators were confined to the school level, while the other three individuals were asked to participate in a number of projects and events beyond the school level. These activities included presenting at district inservice sessions, serving on district committees, facilitating during meetings, working with other schools, and participating in panel discussions on the Project. It is evident that multiple opportunities and multiple perspectives contributed to the learning experience.

Key concerns of the teacher-facilitators centered around time, role clarification, involvement and control, credibility, and conflict. Although some planning and release time was provided for the change facilitators, they were not absolved from any responsibilities in their full-time teaching assignments. Learning to be a change facilitator commanded a great deal of personal time. Each of the individuals struggled with trying to figure out what exactly a change facilitator was supposed to do. Clarifying appropriate levels of involvement was also a concern. All participants worried about working with peers, and all felt the pressure of needing to establish credibility with their colleagues. Finally, disagreement over goals, procedures, and roles affected each individual, and the conflicts had to be negotiated.

Change Facilitator Styles: Passive to Confrontational

Style refers to "those skills which are largely natural, even perhaps out of the awareness or control of the change facilitator, but rather a function of the facilitator's personality" (Miles and colleagues 1988, p. 191). The combination of personal characteristics, levels of involvement, and interpersonal behaviors produced a range of styles from passive to confrontational.

The individuals who had *facilitative* and *assertive* qualities about their style seemed more effective in providing guidance and assistance than those who were either too passive or too dominant. Being *nondirective* rather than directive also appeared to be more successful. Confrontation and force on the part of facilitators led to alienation and resistance. It also resulted in limited opportunities to actively engage in facilitation and to learn about facilitating. One individual was passive, and essentially effected little, if any, change in the group situation.

The Influence of Context

Contextual factors were significant for determining both the learning and work experience of the change facilitators. Factors at the school level, factors at the district level, particular people, and participation in a research study influenced the change facilitators during their first year in the role.

School factors were most important. They included opportunity to present and facilitate, conflict situations, role clarification, and facilitator fit. People and conditions at the respective schools either encouraged and supported or inhibited facilitator's action and learning. Some individuals had more opportunities for active participation in the school improvement activities than others. Each facilitator faced conflict with others some time during the year. The way these conflicts were managed provided for opportunities or constraints to learning. Each facilitator was faced with negotiating his or her role in a particular context. This was a major issue for everyone and, in one case, was never resolved. Clarifying the differences and similarities between the roles and responsibilities of the change facilitator and those of the leadership team created confusion and consumed energy. Also significant was facilitator fit, the elusive match between the style of the facilitator and the site. A set of district factors provided a support structure for the Project and facilitated the learning process. These included the team structure, larger facilitator group, Project coordinators, training, and opportunities for involvement. The facilitators considered both the structured training events and the regular meetings with other learners crucial to their learning. They identified sharing, problem solving, and learning together as key factors.

Facilitators relied on the support and encouragement of particular people throughout the year. The researcher and one of the coordinators were mentioned most often, but other change facilitators, members of the leadership teams, and husbands were also identified.

Participating in a research study during the first year had an impact on the teachers' learning. The journal writing and interviews focused and structured their learning. They noted that the researcher contributed to individual learning in a number of ways: as role model, as problem-solver, as resource person, as trainer, as mentor, and as a friend.

GUIDELINES FOR PRACTICE: SELECTING, TRAINING, AND ASSIGNING FACILITATORS

A number of guidelines can be offered to guide school districts in the selection, training, and assigning of teacher leaders as change facilitators.

Selecting Facilitators

Perhaps one of the most important learnings from this study is the need for role clarification. Defining expectations and articulating the responsibilities of change facilitators is the first step in the selection process. A clear role description will help both facilitators and clients to understand the work of change facilitators. It will also provide direction for those charged with the task of selecting facilitators in choosing the best potential candidates.

Several criteria can be suggested to guide the selection of facilitators. Individuals who see themselves as co-learners in the process seem to be more acceptable and more successful in facilitating change than those we normally might select who have directive leadership qualities. Adaptability and flexibility are key. Facilitating requires the ability to work with a wide range of people who have diverse and varied styles. Personal characteristics and style can not be underestimated. While facilitators can learn knowledge and skills, their basic style and behavior in groups is much more difficult to change. Those with facilitative, assertive, and indirect ways of working with people might be best suited to the role. Caution should be exercised in choosing individuals who are overly forceful, dominating, and directive or very passive and low-key. Effective facilitation is a subtle, quiet process of encouraging individuals to grow and develop and work with others in more productive and effective ways. It requires a delicate balance of pressure and support on the part of assisters.

Facilitator Training

The provision of training for change facilitators is crucial. Preparation for the role and ongoing sessions for networking, problem solving, and continued learning are strongly recommended. Change facilitators cannot be prepared in a short period of time. Both initial and ongoing training need to be comprehensive and intensive. Time is a key issue. School districts choosing to use teacher-facilitators in their improvement efforts need to seriously consider the impact and implications of properly prepared versus inadequately trained facilitators.

Change facilitators need a vast knowledge base. An understanding of the change process and research on school change and change facilitators provides a foundation. Other areas about which facilitators need knowledge include adult learning, organization development, group dynamics, human behavior and motivation, and the particular innovation (school improvement in this case). Also helpful would be an introduction to the literature on the culture of the workplace and the influence of contextual factors on learning.

Facilitating requires a repertoire of skills and strategies. Establishing trust and rapport and role negotiation are crucial skills that individuals require for interacting with clients. Facilitators need to learn skills for role clarification as well as appropriate facilitating behaviors. Task skills and strategies necessary for facilitating change include diagnostic skills, planning and design skills, presentation skills, effective meeting techniques, decision-making procedures, group process skills, and monitoring and evaluation strategies. Some of the people skills that are vital to effective facilitation are teambuilding, conflict resolution, communication, and coaching.

A combination of approaches is recommended to help individuals learn the skills and strategies of facilitating. An in-depth training institute is recommended to provide a foundation for prospective change facilitators. This should be followed by formal, organized sessions at regular intervals during which facilitators can share, problem solve, and continue to learn. Skill training sessions where individuals would have the opportunity to practice and receive feedback on specific skills would also be very useful. Facilitators need to read about the range of topics identified, and journal writing helps them to articulate their learnings and to reflect on their role and the various activities and events with clients.

Finally, coaching is proposed. Pairing new facilitators with experienced facilitators in a mentoring relationship is strongly recommended. Each facilitator needs a coach or supervisor to help them learn the skills of facilitation at the beginning. Facilitating is a complex process, and the problems and appropriate interventions are contextually specific. Immediate assistance and support contributes immeasurably to the learning process.

Assigning Facilitators

Careful consideration must be given to the assignment of change facilitators during their first year. New facilitators are similar to beginning teachers in some respects. Difficult assignments and mismatching contribute to the problems they encounter. Both the change facilitator needs and the client needs should be evaluated in the placement.

The personal mix seems to be an important factor. Of particular significance will be the fit of the facilitator style and basic orientation with that of the administrator and key individuals in the school or organization where they will be working. Role clarification and the careful selection of individuals to be change facilitators will contribute to the reduction of personal conflicts that can inhibit the improvement process.

The culture of the workplace is a second factor that warrants attention in the placement of facilitators. A better understanding of the values and patterns of interaction in the organization will allow for more appropriate matching of facilitators and clients. Placing a strong facilitator with particular values into a situation with others who hold equally strong contradictory beliefs will most likely result in a great deal of conflict and very little actual change. This consideration is of particular significance when individuals are just learning a new role, since they are less able to flex and adapt to the situation. Interviews between facilitators and clients would also promote more effective relationships.

The concept of an internal-external facilitator team is another suggestion to consider. In this design, a local change facilitator from outside the school is paired with an individual or team inside. The two work in concert to encourage and support innovation. A second design for team facilitating pairs two change facilitators in the same school or two schools during their first year. This would provide support, the exchange of ideas, alternate perspectives, and a built-in mechanism for coaching.

CHANGE FACILITATOR: ONE ROLE FOR TEACHER LEADERS

Teachers have many roles to play in the introduction, implementation, and institutionalization of innovations and changes in schools. The change facilitator role is one alternative for teacher leadership. Although some teachers may not be suited to provide leadership from this position and can better make their contribution in other ways, many strong individuals can influence the restructuring of schools by learning about and facilitating problem solving and decision making among their colleagues. The viability and success of this form of teacher leadership will be related to the careful selection, training, and support of individuals to play the particular role of change facilitator.

FOOTNOTE

1. This research was supported by funds from the Social Science and Humanities Research Council of Canada.

REFERENCES

Kilcher, C. A. 1991. Learning to be a change facilitator: A multi-case study. Unpublished doctoral dissertation, University of Maryland, College Park.

Miles, M. B.; Saxl, E. R.; and Lieberman, A. 1988. What skills do educational change agents need? An empirical view. *Curriculum Inquiry* 18(2): 157–193.

Chapter 4

TEACHER LEADERSHIP
IN A RENEWING SCHOOL

by Lynne Miller

The faculty at Narragansett School is committed to transforming their school into a center of inquiry. This commitment has led to new leadership roles for teachers, both planned (positional) and emergent, as the faculty works to restructure their school through a continuous process of questioning, reflecting, and learning. As teachers feel comfortable as learners and leaders, they begin to transform their vision into reality—the school as a center of inquiry for their students.

Narragansett School is a K–3 primary school in Gorham, Maine, a small town located just west of Portland. Gorham has been, until recently, primarily a farming community. In the last five years professional people have settled in the town, adding a bit of suburban flavor. Gorham is also the home of one of the campuses of the University of Southern Maine.

The Gorham school district has two K–3 buildings, one 4–6 school, a junior high school, and a high school. Narragansett is the largest of these schools, having a population of over 500 students and 65 staff. For the past five years, the Gorham schools have been members of the Southern Maine Partnership, a school-university collaboration that is part of John Goodlad's National Network For Educational Renewal. The Partnership's basic unit is the reflective action seminar group, where educators meet monthly to share a reading and to take time to reflect on classroom and school practices. Narragansett teachers have been particularly active in the Early Childhood Group, and its principal has been a core member of the Administrative Leadership Group.

The administrative leadership in the district has been very strong and progressive for the last seven years. The Superintendent is committed to soliciting and using teacher input. She has involved teachers in decision making at a variety of levels, from policy formulation to curriculum development, to daily operations of the schools. Teachers have been encouraged to seek information from outside the school and have drawn on the resources of the local university, more distant institutions of higher education, speakers, and professional publications. Teachers state:

> We have also listened to our own voices. We have participated in an innovative grant that focused on raising the teacher's voice by means of tape recording discussion sessions, getting transcripts for review, and participating in non-grade level discussions. We believe that teachers have a basis of tacit knowledge about classroom practices and children's learning that needs to be built into the structure of schooling. Somehow we must find time to encourage and ultimately to expect teachers to reflect and to share what they know about how children learn and what is important to learn. (Narragansett 1988, p.13)

In the fall of 1988, Narragansett School was notified it had been awarded a three year grant from the State to support its efforts to restructure. Driving these efforts is Robert Schaefer's (1967) notion of "the school as a center of inquiry," a setting where experienced teachers are continuously engaged in the production and use of knowledge and the improvement of practice through disciplined, intentional inquiry. Narragansett's vision of itself is as a school, "serious in purpose, joyous in accomplishment . . . where teachers are more than technicians. They are those who instruct, engage in thoughtful reflection, who seek out research and conduct their own, and who regularly work with colleagues" (Narragansett 1988, p. 5). This vision

116

assumes organizational and individual change. The organization needs to develop new roles and responsibilities for teachers; individuals need to adapt to the new requirements of their roles and to the new demands of the setting.

This chapter[1] traces the development of teacher leadership at Narragansett School since the initiation of the restructuring grant in September 1988. It is best seen as a work in progress. Data were collected through interviews and focus groups, as well as extensive field notes taken by an in-house "scribe," a person hired through the grant to document the change process of the school as it moved toward its vision of becoming a "center of inquiry." Documents were also collected and analyzed. This paper is part of an ongoing study, involving the school staff, which will follow the change process at Narragansett School for three years (the life of the grant).

GETTING STARTED: FORMALIZING TEACHER LEADERSHIP

As the Narragansett staff began planning for restructuring, they "knew we were redefining the teacher role . . . and that in a center of inquiry you cannot continue to add new roles and positions without taking something away" (Narragansett 1988). They had just secured funding from the Gorham School Committee to support five team leader positions. These team leaders were to participate in the management and the educational leadership of the school. They were paid a stipend for their work and were given one-half-day per week as release time. The establishment of such a position was indication of a major shift in the school over the last few years. "We used to feel that everyone should be the same, teach the same. .. We are more comfortable now recognizing that this cannot or will not be the case. If we truly value differences, then we value that change will come from doing things or thinking of things differently" (Narragansett 1988).

In fall 1988, the team leaders began to function in the school. Grade level teachers wrote the description for the role, which included assuming responsibility for communication, representing team views, disseminating information, coordinating budgets, designating committee representation, supervising field trips, overseeing mentorships for new teachers, and scheduling and coordinating the use of teacher assistants. Selection of team leaders was left to the teachers in each team, which were organized by grade level. The kindergarten, first, and third grade teacher selected the one volunteer who was interested; the second grade team drew a name from a hat because three teachers were interested in the position. The early team leader meetings were dominated by concerns about clarifying the role, connecting with resources, and learning to work as leaders individually with other teachers and collectively as a leadership group.

Now in its second year, the team leader position is established in the school. Struggles with time, leadership skills, and working in a role as it is being defined were identified in the first year and continued into the next, though these struggles seem to be the almost exclusive concerns of those in the team leader positions. Most other faculty accept the management and leadership functions of the team leader position and acknowledge its effectiveness in school operations.

It is interesting to note that team leaders have worked in ways that go beyond their specified job descriptions. They develop agendas for grade level and team leader meetings, address the unplanned-for issues in daily school routines, seek out and make available timely articles from professional journals, build time for discussion with team members, and offer personal and professional assistance to their teaching colleagues. Now, well into their second year, the team leaders seem to have created a niche for themselves that is more beholden to and in the service of other teachers than to the administration.

EXPLORING NEW TERRITORY: EMERGENT TEACHER LEADERSHIP

An early working assumption of the Narragansett restructuring project was that teachers in a school as a center of inquiry would begin to ask questions and generate answers about the nature of student learning and that these activities would lead to new ways of thinking about and organizing instruction in the school. It was further assumed that as teachers became comfortable with the notions of open inquiry and reflection on practice, they would initiate new ways of doing things. It was not clear, however, in the early days of the grant, just how these new approaches would emerge and who would assume responsibility for developing them.

By the end of the first year of the grant, fully one half of the teaching staff had become involved in new teaching arrangements. By September 1989 the following new arrangements were in place:

- a kindergarten program where teachers involved in early kindergarten and regular kindergarten were working together as a team;

- a first grade teacher moved with her students into second grade;

- a first and a second grade teacher combined their classes and offered a multigrade 1–2 classroom;

- a second and third grade teacher combined to form a 2–3 grade class in the morning; they were joined by the 1–2 grade team for the afternoon, so that after lunch they had a 1–3 classroom, team taught by four teachers;

- two second grade teachers combined their classes and team taught a larger second grade section;

- a third grade teacher teamed with a composite resource

119

room teacher to offer a classroom, which fully integrated special needs and standard students.

In each instance, teachers, usually working together, developed ideas about changing their self-contained classrooms and then put their ideas into practice. While much of the discussion among teachers took place in the formal grade level meetings, it was classroom teachers, not the designated team leaders, who initiated the change efforts. Leadership in program development and curriculum reform had emerged from patterns of interaction that had taken root in the school. A process of inquiry, dialogue, reflection, invention, and action was becoming the modus operandi of the school. The new organizational arrangements had not been planned as an outcome of the restructuring grant; they grew out of the questions, concerns, and dialogue of the staff. Leadership for school change did not come from those in formally designated roles as might be expected; it emerged from the ranks of classroom teachers, seeking to improve their practices.

This emergent teacher leadership became normative in the school. Staff development moved away from the workshop model and began to offer teacher-led sessions during the district's allotted in-service days. One teacher has assumed leadership among her colleagues in discussions about theories of learning and thinking, drawing on the work of Gardner and Sternberg. Another has taken responsibility for leading a re-examination of the early-kindergarten/kindergarten program. Others have come forward to spearhead school and district-wide curriculum development efforts.

Perhaps the most dramatic example of emergent teacher leadership is in the area of student assessment. The acknowledgment of knowledge and expertise in this domain was motivated by an external source. The Mastery In Learning Project of the National Education Association had contacted the Director of the Southern Maine Partnership in search of a school where teachers were doing something different in terms of student learning and assessment. The Mastery In Learning Project was directed to the principal of Narragansett School, who agreed to invite her staff to make a presentation at a national conference. Three teachers volunteered to work with the principal to develop the presentation. By committing to a public appearance, the teachers had also committed to working together to make the school's tacit knowledge and evolving practices explicit and comprehensible to a wider audience. The assessment group reached out to the general faculty for assistance. Slides were taken, a script written, parts assigned, and a final product developed and refined. The Mastery In Learning presentation was well-received, and the Narragansett teachers gained an immediate reputation as experts in alternative forms of assessment. The original group has presented throughout the state as well as in other parts of the country. Without benefit of title or degree, the teachers involved have gained recognition as experts in the field of student assessment.

INVENTING NEW POSSIBILITIES:
THE TEACHER-SCHOLAR POSITION

As the second year of the grant draws to a close, the Narragansett School is proposing a newly funded position, that of teacher-scholar. The teacher-scholar will be a staff person who will take a sabbatical for a full year within the school setting. The job of the teacher-scholar will be to pursue a topic for investigation and research.

The first mention of teacher-scholar is in the original grant, but there it is a fuzzy concept at best, tied to the notion of the "school as a center of inquiry" but with no mention of what the teacher-scholars do or how they do it. As the principal noted:

When we wrote the grant, we wrote about the teacher as scholar. But we didn't decide to create this position. It had to emerge from our understanding and our need. We knew that a scholarship and research orientation isn't like margarine, something you can spread all over. (Fieldnotes 1988–1990)

121

What happened over the course of the two years of the grant was that people began to surface who had research and scholarly concerns about practice. A teacher from the integrated Special/Ed/Standard team became intrigued by the notion of intelligence and metacognition and their implications for teaching and assessment. The second grade teacher, who brought her first graders with her, raised questions about how children respond to different approaches to reading in her classroom. Four teachers working in a nongraded team wanted to track how children of different ages interacted with each other and with the curriculum. As these teachers discussed their ideas with their colleagues and with the principal, there grew a consensus among a large portion of the staff that something had to be done to accommodate these new and compelling interests. The principal noted:

> What emerged made sense—to have projects you want to deal with. Every year, I ask for an assistant principal, but there are better things to ask for. My heart is never in it. I knew there was a better way to run the building, but wasn't sure yet. It seemed important to create a new role—someone who can give educational leadership from within, who has an interest in a project or product. The teacher-scholar position surfaced and I pursued it with the Board because this time my heart was in it. (Fieldnotes 1988–1990)

The School Board voted to fund the teacher-scholar position for the 1990-91 school year.

THE DEVELOPMENT OF TEACHER LEADERSHIP

The concept and practice of teacher leadership are still evolving at Narragansett School. An initial stab at charting the evolution of teacher leadership looks like this:

1. The restructuring grant begins with the assumption that teacher roles will change.

122

2. The formalized role of the team leader is established as in-grade level organization, supported by an extra stipend and release time. The role gains acceptance.

3. Teachers develop new programs outside of, but facilitated by, the formal team leader role and the formal grade level structure.

4. As programs develop, teachers see the need to test their new organizational arrangements and their new practices.

5. Some teachers develop questions that require time and systematic investigation to answer.

6. The role of a rotating teacher-scholar is proposed.

What distinguishes teacher leadership at Narragansett School from other documented efforts in this regard is its evolutionary and open nature. Much of the current literature (Little 1988; Wasley 1991) relates the possibilities and problems of teacher leadership when it is construed as a formal or assigned role within the school. At Narragansett, the team leader role is a starting point for teacher leadership, but it is clearly not the end point.

Two questions about teacher leadership at Narragansett seem worthy of exploring. What accounts for its course of development? Is there a connection between teacher leadership in the school and what happens in classrooms?

Accounting for Teacher Leadership

A partial explanation for the course of teacher leadership at Narragansett lies in the ethos of the school district, as developed and nurtured by the Superintendent. She had clearly set the stage for teacher professionalism and participation in instructional decisions, and she communicated her expectations and her trust frequently and unambiguously.

One thing is clear to us. . . . The teacher is key to fundamental improvement. What he or she knows and can implement regarding subject matter, child development, and the craft of teaching is critical. . . . Any attempt at restructuring will support, expect, and attempt to enlarge upon the efforts of able and dedicated teachers. (Goldman 1988)

The superintendent provided material, as well as verbal support. She lobbied for more teaching assistants to free teachers from clerical and custodial duties; she promoted the team leader concept and supported it with time and money; she bargained for increased staff development; she encouraged teachers to attend outside conferences and events; she supported teachers' taking courses at the university; she engaged noted speakers in the areas of teaching and learning; she arranged for teacher seminars at universities inside and outside of Maine; she engaged noted speakers in the areas of teaching and learning; and finally she visited classrooms regularly and engaged teachers in conversation about what they were teaching, how they were teaching, and why it was worth teaching.

Another key to understanding teacher leadership at Narragansett is the role that the principal played. A former teacher at the school, the principal quickly established herself as a teacher-advocate and as someone with a compelling vision. She promoted the idea of the "school as a center of inquiry" consistently and unrelentingly; she made clear that while teachers did not have to agree on instructional practices, they did have to be able to question what they did and why they did it. She publicly valued the giving of reason. For example, when the principal observed a teacher assigning children the task of memorizing the presidents of the United States, she didn't criticize the approach but rather asked why the teacher made the assignment. When the teacher explained the pride that children showed when they had mastered the task and how she assured every student the opportunity to achieve mastery, the principal acknowledged the value of the lesson and indicated that she was more interested in the reasons the teacher gave for what she did than she was in the practice itself (Fieldnotes 1988–1990). By interacting with teachers in this way, the principal won their trust in her pronouncements that there was no one best way to teach, and that diverse styles would be valued at Narragansett, so long as teachers could give reasons for what they did.

The principal articulated and defended the vision of the "school as a center of inquiry" at every opportunity. In her mind, inquiry meant being open to questions, investigation, and to possibilities. She saw restructuring as continuous and ongoing, "a never-ending story. What we do now isn't *it*. It's *it* for right now, but not forever" (Fieldnotes 1988–1990). In the same vein, she viewed teacher leadership as generative:

> I'm glad we did the team leader thing. It shared struggles and concerns and it showed that teacher leadership is real. But, you don't stop there. You don't say, we have team leaders; now let's forget it and get on with business. Rather you allow things to be questioned and to happen that will evolve into other ways for teachers to assume different kinds of leadership. Teacher leadership, like restructuring, is a self-correcting community of scholars.

The other crucial factor in the evolution of teacher leadership at Narragansett is the habit of reflective practice that the teachers in the school embraced and developed over time. The restructuring team wrote in the original grant proposal:

> We have read Schon's *Reflective Practitioner,* looked at McDonald's work on raising the teacher's voice and Shulman's thinking about developing a coherent theory of practice. The metaphor of school-as-center-of-inquiry comes from a 1967 address by Robert Schaefer. (Narragansett 1988, p. 9)

Further, they noted:

> This vision has not been intrinsically concerned nor has it been

125

based on a specific model—instead it has come from years of thinking about things differently. It is based on the premise that it is not only acceptable, but a professional responsibility to challenge the status-quo and to seek a better way. (Narragansett 1988, p. 9)

Teachers at the school had been afforded opportunities to "think about things differently" well before the grant began. As active members of the Early Childhood Group of the Southern Maine Partnership, over half the staff met monthly with other educators and university faculty to challenge conventional notions of practice. As participants in the district's Early Childhood Task Force, they were encouraged to re-think and re-design primary education. In close proximity to the university, many teachers took advantage of courses and degree programs focused on instructional leadership. Several teachers came to the restructuring effort with privately nurtured intellectual interests already in place. They were able to talk to others, influence their peers, and contribute to the school's development without being resented or undermined.

My work at Narragansett School leads me to conclude that a culture of questioning, inquiry, reflection, experimentation, and trust developed among the faculty. This was promoted by a strong district commitment, to teacher professionalism, participatory school leadership, opportunities for dialog and action; and, lastly, the unique talents and interests of the teachers in the school. This last element is the most elusive.

Connecting Teacher Leadership and Classroom Practices

Teacher leadership is not an end in itself. It is, rather, a necessary condition for renewed professionalism and ultimately for the improvement of educational practices that affect children. As Myrna Cooper reminds us:

In the final analysis, there is no professional culture for teachers save what is conferred through their students. If participation in the profession, in decision making, in the rites of power and control helps children, then a professional culture will have meaning. That being the benchmark, the effort will not be self-serving. (Cooper 1988, p. 54)

When teachers at Narragansett were asked directly about the relationship between teacher leadership and classroom instruction, they spoke of a renewed concern about learning and teaching:

Even though we have known all along how important feelings about ourselves as learners affects our learning—I say, if this affects me this much, then everything I do with a child must come from his feelings about himself. Because someone who values and respects what I am now affects my learning, I am giving my best energy to teaching. (Fieldnotes 1988–1990)

This renewal was rooted in feelings of self-esteem that were developing in the school:

We started believing in ourselves and what we were doing. The atmosphere created that. I have been teaching for 18 years and now I have excitement about my work. I feel more relaxed because I feel good about what I am doing.

You are more relaxed because you have more confidence in yourself. We are not teaching the textbook because we are told to teach it. We are given flexibility in what we do. We now work with our capabilities.

You develop a sense of self esteem, of personal dignity, a sense of personal wealth and then you develop those things in your children. (Fieldnotes 1988–1990)

Teachers clearly recognized the connection between their own development and the development of the children they taught.

Teachers also made the connection between their increased role in decision making and providing more choices to their students:

Kids can learn the same things, but they can choose what is best for them. For example, I now ask, how can kids plan for the week? Instead of setting down with my plan book on Sunday night, I can now brainstorm with the kids—what do we have to do this week?

I tend to value the children as decision makers more. (Fieldnotes 1988–1990)

As these comments indicate, when teachers felt valued as members of a coherent community, and empowered as decision makers, they were able to empower their students by offering them choices and by including them in decisions affecting their own instruction.

Finally, teachers linked their reflection and inquiry about learning with a willingness to engage students in thinking about thinking, inviting them to view the learning process as daring, exciting, complicated, and personal:

I am at a point where I know it is important to tell children why we are doing something. I also encourage them to be risk-takers more than ever before. Take a chance, that is how you learn. I say so frequently, "You learn by making mistakes!" That has never been my motto before.

I encourage children to see that there are often multiple right answers.

I give the children a chance to talk about their learning.

I recognize multiple models of good teaching. This leads to an understanding that there is not one best way to learn— for us or for the children. I tell them that. (Fieldnotes 1988–1990)

This connection between teacher learning and student learning was particularly powerful for the teachers at Narragansett School. They referred to it often in their interviews and in conversation.

This discussion of Narragansett School began with a description of its vision as a center of inquiry, a place where teachers and students were engaged in a continuous process of questioning, reflecting, and learning. It seems fair to conclude that this vision helped promote leadership roles for teachers that were both formal and informal, planned and emergent, and that as teachers felt comfortable as learners and as leaders, they began to transform the vision into reality for themselves and for their students.

NOTE

1. This chapter was originally presented as a paper at the American Educational Research Association annual meeting in Boston, MA, April 16, 1990.

REFERENCES

Fieldnotes. 1988-1990. Fieldnotes from Narragansett School.

Goldman, C. 1988. What is this thing called restructuring? Unpublished manuscript.

Little, J. W. 1988. Assessing the prospects for teacher leadership. In *Building a professional culture in schools,* ed. A. Lieberman, 78–106. New York: Teachers College Press.

Narragansett. 1988. Narragansett school proposal to the state of Maine.

Schaefer, R. 1967. *The school as a center of inquiry.* New York: Harper and Row.

Schon, D. 1983. *The reflective practitioner: How professionals think in practice.* New York: Basic Books.

Wasley, P. 1991. The practical work of teacher leaders: Assumptions, attitudes, and acrophobia. In *Staff development: New demands, new realities, new perspectives, 2d ed.,* ed. A. Lieberman and L. Miller. New York: Teachers College Press.

Chapter 5

LEADING, LEARNING, AND LEAVING

by Susan Walters
with Cynthia Guthro

Two teacher leaders reflect on the circumstances and effects of their leadership roles in a school that is restructuring toward shared decision making and inquiry. Teacher leadership affected their relationships with teaching peers, their sense of self-as-teacher, and their students' learning experiences. Learnings from their experience include: Teacher leadership requires collaboration with peers; "voice" is essential for risk-taking and inquiry; and leading may require "leaving" or "letting go"—with peers, to encourage collaboration and leadership across the faculty, and with students, to become facilitators of learning rather than givers of information.

- What circumstances propel individuals to assume leadership?

- What roles do teacher-leaders assume?

- How does leadership affect one's view of oneself as a teacher?

- How does leadership affect relations with peers?

- What is its impact on the classroom?

Four years of a restructuring project have given the staff of Wells Junior High School experience with teacher leadership, but few definitive answers to these questions. In the dialogue

131

recorded in this article, two of us who have become teacher-leaders share our experiences, hoping that our reflections may contribute some understanding to the questions posed.

We make no claim that our stories constitute generalizable research. Rather, they illustrate what Lieberman and Miller (1986) describe as "the real messiness and idiosyncratic nature of the real stories of school improvement" (p. 6). McDonald (1986) considers the telling of stories the first step in breaking the long silence of teachers isolated in the individual classrooms of the "cellular school." The finding of a voice by teachers "can contribute to school policy essential knowledge that is available from no other source" (p. 360). The dialogue was constructed primarily from a series of interviews and conversations that took place in early summer 1990. Cindy read and commented on each of the several drafts, making corrections and additions.

Since leadership develops within a context, some explanation of our common history is needed. The history of Wells Junior High began in 1977, when the district built a new high school and created a separate junior high in the old high school building. By 1985, it had matured into an effective, traditional junior high school, with a hierarchical decision-making structure, and a reliance on lecture, seatwork, and worksheets as primary instructional strategies.

In 1986, Wells Junior High became part of the Mastery In Learning (MIL) project, an NEA-sponsored network for school renewal. The project empowered school faculties to create the climate and conditions necessary for staff and students to restructure their schools into self-renewing centers of inquiry. MIL was not intended as a prescriptive "package" for school improvement. Instead, project director Bob McClure emphasized the principle that every decision about teaching and learning that can be made by a local school faculty must be made by that faculty. Decision making should be informed by educational research, applied in the light of teachers' own experiences and knowledge of their unique setting.

At the beginning of the project, our staff and other representatives of the school community participated in a needs assessment. Communications and grouping of students for instruction were selected as priority areas for improvement. These two areas formed the springboard for change. Over a period of four years, we developed a consensus decision making process which involves the whole staff, a way of working together which honors the thinking of all individuals in the school. Leadership is shared, and new leadership roles, both formal and informal, have evolved. For example, leadership for staff meetings is provided on a rotating basis by teams of volunteers. Change has become an ongoing evolutionary process which involves us all as a community and for which we all take responsibility. We have made changes which fundamentally improve school for our students.

We, the two speakers, began working at Wells Junior High on the same day in February 1977. Although we both taught at the same grade level for most of the ensuing thirteen years, we didn't collaborate, in spite of the close relations between our content areas, language arts and reading. We have very different teaching styles and personalities, and our leadership roles have followed different paths. At the time of this conversation, Cindy was teaching reading on the grade 8 team and serving as team leader. Sue was serving as Certification Teacher, a two-year K-12 position which includes responsibilities for a peer support process for new teachers and district staff development.

WHAT CIRCUMSTANCES PROPEL AN INDIVIDUAL TO ASSUME LEADERSHIP?

Our first leadership opportunities were not unlike those found in schools across the United States—subject area coordinator and association leadership.

Cindy: A leadership role I had prior to MIL was as the reading

133

coordinator for the junior high. I was involved in budgeting and trying to develop a reading curriculum scope and sequence. I also tried, where I could, to help the two new reading teachers we had that year. I tried to have regular department meetings, but without much success. Even at our infrequent meetings, we never really talked about the program as a grade 6–8 concern. We kicked around some issues, but didn't really resolve much. Mainly, we went into our classrooms and shut the doors. We each did our own thing.

Because I had that title for a while, I felt people saw me as more than just a teacher. I probably had more access to the principal than others because of budget questions. I didn't see any other role; at faculty meetings we just sat and got talked at. The only decisions we made five years ago were what we wanted in our budgets. There were a few committees here and there, but policymaking, planning what we wanted for workshops, we had no voice in things like that.

Sue: We really had little influence beyond our own classrooms. During the first four years of my teaching career, I was totally centered in my classroom, trying to survive, trying to figure out how to make writing meaningful to reluctant students, to manage my classroom. There was no support from administration or other teachers, and I didn't concern myself with what was going on in the school as a whole until an incident which occurred in the spring of my fourth year. I found myself in disagreement with an administrator about a proposed change. Although the entire staff and many parents opposed the particular change, and it was eventually scuttled, two of us were regarded as troublemakers by the administrator, and our dissent was punished. At this time I was asked to become president of WOTA, the local teachers' association. I didn't want to be visible because I was afraid the price was too high.

Cindy: I think a lot of us were angry at the treatment you got from the administration. However, we didn't know what to do, or we were afraid to try anything. The threat was there, that it

134

could happen to us. So we left you on your own. I didn't feel good about that.

Sue: That experience, while painful, had positive results. As president of WOTA, I played a variety of roles. Membership was not very active; the Executive Committee consisted of a few deeply involved individuals. I was part of the Negotiating Committee and also worked on grievances. I attended district meetings of MTA. Two years later, a new superintendent arrived; he was very open to working with the association, and I found my leadership role in the district expanding. I was able to recruit some new members to the negotiating team, and the next contract settlement was viewed as a real step forward by most staff members.

I also spent more time on issues involving potential conflict between association members and the administration, at the request of both groups, thus avoiding potential grievances. I represented the association on hiring committees. I was able to expand the WOTA Executive Committee, which developed into a very good working team. These experiences increased my self-confidence and broadened my frame of reference. I began to see issues on a district level and to understand the perspectives of administrators as well as teachers.

As a result of my association work, I became involved in writing a proposal to pilot the new Maine teacher certification law, which included a mandatory peer support process for new teachers. I was particularly interested in this because of the lack of support we received as new teachers. I also believed that peer support had the potential to involve teachers in collaboration and raise the level of professionalism. Our proposal was successful and we began a peer support process. The training in coaching was sometimes uncomfortable, as it exposed my teaching to the view of my colleagues.

In 1985, the phrase "teacher empowerment" caught my attention in an ad in an NEA publication soliciting applications for the Mastery In Learning project. Because I felt that the impetus of a national project could provide a catalyst for moving the school to a new stage of development, I applied, much in the spirit of buying a lottery ticket. To my great surprise, our school was one of 26 accepted. In order to become part of the Project, 75 percent of the faculty had to vote to participate. With little discussion, the staff voted almost unanimously to become part of MIL. I interpreted the lack of dissent as support; in retrospect, that wasn't so. I realize now that it was regarded as *my* project; and, as long as that remained true, it was doomed to fail.

Looking back, no single event prompted me to seek a leadership role. Rather, it evolved from responses to a series of events and opportunities. I was motivated by a sense that something was missing; I wanted to work within a school that encouraged innovation and collaboration, where teachers talked about teaching and learning, where everything focused on what was best for kids. I believed that teachers should have more say in decision making and was lucky enough to have opportunities to try out that belief. Everything I've experienced has reinforced my conviction that teacher decision making leads to a better school for kids. I've also become very aware of the difficulties involved. It can be done, but it's damned hard.

Cindy: I see the importance now of being involved outside my own classroom, both within the school and within the district. In my position as team leader, my leadership role has evolved. When I began as team leader two years ago, I saw myself as a secretary for my team. Then my role really started to change. We (the team leaders) took on new responsibilities. Issues came up that needed to be dealt with; that's when I really hit my stride. I really felt I was breaking away last year when I was involved in developing the plan to restructure the K-8 administration. I presented our needs as teachers at a public meeting. That was my turning point. I had a feeling that "I'm contributing, and someone is listening." I began to get reinforcement for this idea from comments made by the high school principal and the assistant superintendent. I came to realize I wasn't giving myself enough credit sometimes.

136

Last year a group of us met at my house to develop a mission statement for the junior high. Everyone there was heavily invested in change. The ideas came from teachers, not just administrators. It wasn't us against them either; we worked together. I was the one who presented the draft of the mission statement to the whole staff, and it was accepted.

WHAT ROLES DO TEACHER LEADERS ASSUME?

Leadership development leads some to a more visible role; the desire to facilitate the growth of colleagues may necessitate stepping into a background role for others.

Sue: When our participation in MIL began, I was a very visible leader. I was good at getting things started. But my very visibility was a liability in terms of getting others involved. I had to let go of my original leadership role in order for the change process to work. I really had not thought out what teacher empowerment meant, nor did I understand how to go about developing it. Certainly I didn't envision the changes in my own leadership style that would be required.

The changes didn't occur until the second and third year. During the first year, people were excited about being involved in a national project. There was lots of activity; we had almost three-quarters of the staff involved on at least one MIL committee. The committees accomplished a great deal, but most of those changes were superficial. By Christmas of the second year, we hit a very difficult period. I didn't know enough about the change process to understand that this was normal. I realize now that we were at the point when many people realized that more significant changes would require enormous effort and disrupt our lives. For example, the Grouping Committee spent six months reading the research on homogeneous and heterogeneous grouping. They were charged with making a recommendation about grouping practices for the whole school by November of the second year. In the end, they recommended staying with tracking. I was shocked; it made no sense to me. Here we were, empowering teachers to make decisions about teaching and learning based on research, and the first major decision flew in the face of all the research they had read. The administrators, who believed that the current system was bad for kids psychologically and socially, were equally upset. However, we never talked about overriding that decision.

Marylyn, our new project consultant, had attended all meetings of the committee from September on. She told me that she sensed that committee members were really uneasy with the idea of mixed groups. She described them as a "group working hard at something they didn't believe in." The research was giving them overwhelming evidence that they should propose a change to mixed groups, but they were overwhelmed by the difficulties involved. They themselves were not prepared to make the change; they didn't know how to modify their instructional strategies to work with mixed groups. They knew this was true for the rest of the staff.

I learned some important lessons about leadership from this incident. At the time, I believed that the committee made a selfish, short-sighted decision based on personal needs and fear. Over time I came to understand the wisdom of that decision. Our staff *wasn't* ready to make that major a change. They needed time to learn some ways to teach mixed groups. It would probably have been a disastrous mistake to go ahead. That was the beginning of my learning about the importance of listening to the misgivings of those who are uncomfortable with a particular change, rather than dismissing them as "blockers." Their concerns often give valuable insight into what will and won't work.

I also learned something about patience from this incident, and about letting go of my own ideas about how change should happen. The committee's decision eventually led to some major changes, in a different way from what I had imagined. For several weeks afterward, they talked about what to do next. They knew that the strongest argument against tracking is the equity issue. To address that, they came up with recommendations to provide more rich learning opportunities for all kids, regardless of group. They recommended a change in the schedule which would create an additional period for activities. They also supported a pilot project which would give those teachers who wanted to try some mixed groups an opportunity to do so.

During that year, teachers on the committee began experimenting with cooperative learning and other strategies they'd read about in the grouping research. After much discussion, the staff approved the schedule changes. By the following fall, there was an obvious difference in the way kids were learning. The school was a much more exciting, alive place to be. And heterogeneous grouping did occur that year in Allied Arts and during the activity period.

However, I couldn't see progress at the time. The next five months were awful. People started dropping off committees. At every steering committee meeting people would say that the project was doomed, it was going down the tubes. I was discouraged, but not as pessimistic as some. At times, I felt like a Pollyanna, shallow and not really aware of what was going on. I later understood that it was important for me to remain optimistic. If I had ever been visibly discouraged, it might have really been the end.

Our turning point as a staff came at a two-day workshop in March. We knew we needed a success, and we planned really carefully. Marylyn, our consultant, facilitated. The first day went well. I wasn't there on the second day because my father died during the night. The second day began with business as usual. Part way through the morning, someone stood up and said, "I can't believe that we're just going on like this when Sue's father has just died." Her comment opened the door for a flood of feelings. Almost a third of the staff had been touched by a family death in the past year. Marylyn was able to show the importance of dealing with feelings in a work setting. By the end of the day, the staff had agreed—by consensus—to meet twice monthly for 45 minutes to make decisions together. For a staff used to monthly meetings of 20 minutes, this was a major commitment. It established norms which formed the basis of our working together for the next three years. Over time, we have extended the length of our meetings, and we meet more frequently when needed. It seemed ironic that I wasn't there for such a significant moment in our development, and also that an event in my personal life was a precipitating factor. It also is wonderfully symbolic, since much of what I have learned about leading involves letting go.

Much of my leadership development has involved leaving old roles and old conceptions behind. I've had to do that for the health of things I've started. After working to develop the WOTA executive committee as a working team, the time came when I had to step down as president for that group of new leaders to continue their growth. Although other past presidents remained on the executive committee in an advisory role, I didn't. It was several years before I was informally consulted on association issues. I kept my distance because I had to let go, I had to leave, even though it was painful.

After the March workshop, my leadership role on the junior high staff changed. For a long time, I didn't know what it was, or even if I had a leadership role. I left behind my visibility and wasn't sure what would replace it. Although I was one of the individuals who volunteered to serve as facilitators for staff meetings, it was over six months before I actually did so. I felt that others who had not been visible leaders should facilitate. This was important to establish a norm that facilitating meetings was something everyone could do, not just the people who were leaders in the past. I was also concerned that I wasn't seen as neutral. The steering committee, which I had chaired since the beginning, went through the same identity crisis. All the decisions we made in the past were being made by the whole staff after the March workshop, which was great. However, it didn't look like there was a role for the committee. We talked about disbanding or defining a new role, but didn't do either. Over time, a role emerged from our uncertainty and confusion. I would describe the steering committee as the collective guardian of the staff decision making process. The committee is responsible for making sure that lists of topics for staff meetings are developed and prioritized by the whole group.

My own role is as support person for the process. I frequently help facilitation teams plan the meeting format, and I make sure that needed materials are ready. I sometimes facilitate meetings myself, now, and have gained confidence in my ability to be a neutral facilitator. I've been a spokesperson for the project to the outside world, speaking at conferences and writing about our experiences. My favorite role is facilitating the leadership development of others, which I could not do without leaving behind my old visible role. I've been rewarded for that by watching my colleagues and friends develop their own leadership skills and roles. I thought that some of the people who have since become active leaders would probably never buy into MIL. Cindy, you're an example of that. I always admired your organization and air of confidence, but felt you were pretty conservative about changing. Seeing how much you've changed and grown has been a wonderful privilege. It's also humbling to realize how much impact someone's "crazy idea" can have on individual lives.

Cindy: At first, I didn't know what to think when you and Marylyn started to come to me for my opinions, to be a spokesperson for certain viewpoints in staff meetings. You said people would listen more to something if it came from me. I never felt like people felt that way about me. You said I presented a neutral view. My perception of myself at that time is that I had a more conservative outlook. I tried to be fair, but I adopted a "wait and see" stance at first.

Now I see myself as having two priorities. The first, as it has always been, is doing the best job I can in my classroom, making sure I understand what I'm doing and why I'm doing it. My second priority, a fairly new one, is to protect what I've come to see as my (and others') rights. I want to have a voice and I want to keep it. I want that voice to count for something. I feel this strongly now. Before MIL I didn't feel this way, and I don't think many others did either. That's probably because we didn't know what having a voice could mean. We would bitch and gripe a lot about decisions that were handed down. We'd either follow them or try to get around them—go through the motions. And, thinking back on it, the decisions that got sabotaged were usually not very good ones in the first place. Certainly, not many of us were invested in them.

When we first knew we could make decisions as a faculty, we were scared. Some decisions turned out to be bad ones, and we couldn't hide in our rooms or snicker in the faculty room and point to an administrator saying, "I told you so."

There are pluses and minuses to participatory decision making. The most difficult factor for me—and I would guess for many other staff members—is the time element. We can beat issues to death. Then we resurrect them and beat them again. But, in the end, these time-consuming discussions lead to changes that last and that make a difference. So that's also a positive factor.

Personally, it's frustrating when I want a change and it's not forthcoming. I've been thinking how great it would be if every staff development day this coming year was to be used to learn teaching strategies for heterogeneous groups. At the end of the year, we'd each, personally, have developed a month's worth of units—classroom and interdisciplinary—ready to go in the fall. But this can't be mandated. It needs to come from us, and some of us aren't ready yet. I guess one of my new roles is going to be gently lobbying for change in this direction.

Sue: Mandating a change like that would be a lot easier. We could avoid a lot of conflict. That's part of what takes so much time. But one of the most important lessons I've learned from this whole experience is that conflict is healthy and necessary. It always existed; it just got talked about in the parking lot instead of at staff meetings. When people didn't agree with something, they found other ways to get their feelings across, or they just found ways not to do it. Now we know what people are thinking, and we work through their objections or concerns, so when we reach a decision together, we know that none of us will sabotage it. Encouraging people to express disagreement is an important part of my role now, although I sure didn't see it that way when we started. I felt challenged when someone disagreed with one of my "great ideas" and thought I had to defend it. Now I know that when staff members raise concerns or objections, that's really helpful. They know best the problems that will occur. By listening to them and taking their concerns into account, we'll have a much better plan. I used to think of the objectors as "swamp people," as blockers. Now I understand their contribution to this school community. They keep the "idea people," who might be driving the wagon over the cliff on a weekly basis, firmly grounded in reality. We need to have everyone express their views. That gives shared decision making its strength.

Cindy: Even though I understand the importance of being involved in decision making, I still see my primary focus as the classroom for a while. I'll be team leader for one more year. I do see myself as being more open to trying other new roles. I recently agreed to speak at a national conference sponsored by the College Board on providing equal access to education for minority students. I never could have seen myself doing something like that. I was scheduled to speak on the second day. I kept hearing comments about *white, middle-class female teachers* and the way they reinforce inequities for minority students. It made me angry. I closed my speech by telling them that I'm that white middle-class teacher, and I'm feeling a bit embattled. I told them that most teachers I know recognize that their roles are changing. Most of us want to try to make a difference in kids' lives. Most teachers I know are willing to make changes necessary for all kids to reach their potential, but we need the time, training, and support necessary to carry out those changes. My presentation was really well received. Several people asked for a copy of my remarks, and quite a few thanked me for speaking up for teachers. I never could have seen myself doing something like this a few years ago.

I have more to learn about working with heterogeneous groups. Then I'm thinking about *taking my show on the road.* I'll reach the point where I can share with others. The idea is in the back of my mind that I may have something worth sharing with others. But I don't see myself moving out of the classroom yet; I have too many things I want to try. Until I'm bored. I'll stay here, and I haven't been bored yet.

I was stagnating back then, and I knew it, but I didn't know what to do. Those great observations I got: I was fooling everyone but myself. It wasn't that I was a bad teacher. I look back and understand that the way I would judge myself as a teacher then and now is very different. I was pretty tough on myself. I've had to relax, to let go of a lot of notions of what a *good teacher* has to do. I began to do this after the workshop two years ago, when Lynne Miller and Cherie Foster talked with us about the research on the needs of adolescents. I realized, "I'm not doing those things." It's important for me to share my reactions. People get a picture that they can't change, or it doesn't matter what they do. I didn't know if cooperative learning would work when I first tried it, but I knew I had to do something. If there's any lesson to be learned, it's this: Just *do* something; make a step somehow.

HOW DOES LEADERSHIP AFFECT RELATIONS WITH PEERS?

Teachers taking on leadership roles are often held suspect by colleagues.

Cindy: I wondered, "How can she [Sue] take on so many things and do them all?" I couldn't have done it. I always thought you were an excellent teacher, because you tried so many things. I tended to be—as one of my principals once told me—a "stuffed

144

shirt traditionalist." I'm sure he meant that in the nicest way!

Sue: I sometimes felt people thought I wanted to do too much.

Cindy: I agree. I would think "If she wants to do it, good for her. Let her go for it, but she'd better not rattle my cage." I think there was also some question about your motives. When someone promotes something new, there's always a question about what they are doing it for. There must be something hidden, a desire for personal gain. People wondered what you were up to.

Sue: It's easy to see it as a stepping stone. I certainly have benefitted from my involvement, but that wasn't my primary motive.

Cindy: Even if it was, and it was something that would be for the good of the school, then it should be OK. But people lose sight of that. When it's a big change, people get nervous. They get annoyed. You have to admit, we'd been through so many changes here, and they ended up being put in a filing cabinet and forgotten. On the heels of ECRI and Precision Teaching, this seemed like one more crazy idea. We'd gotten rid of the last principal and his crazy idea.

I don't think people knew what to think of you back then. We thought you had your own motivations. We knew about your problems with the last principal. We saw you working with the association; and then you put the Mastery In Learning project on your plate. A lot of people resented you, although I don't think I did. Some were concerned about the investment of time. Then, when we found out that we had to raise our own funding to participate, we wondered, "What kind of a Mickey Mouse outfit is this?" You were still in the classroom and doing all this. People wondered—me included—how can she do all this and teach? The rest of us had enough trouble keeping it together in our classrooms. People either respected you or thought you were real ditzy. They couldn't take a neutral stand on you.

Sue: A concern for me was balancing my role as a teacher and my leadership responsibilities. Sometimes I felt guilty, because I was afraid I wasn't putting enough energy into my classroom. I felt a greater responsibility to be an effective teacher, so I tried even harder to do a good job, to be innovative, to reach every kid. Trying to do both was exhausting. At the same time, it was often exhilarating.

Cindy: Some people may have thought you were grabbing at power. Last spring, when we were deciding on who would become acting principal for the last three months of school, your name was suggested. The staff wasn't ready for that. It was such an enormous step out of the teacher role: too much, too fast. People felt we were in an avalanche of change at that point, and we just kept rolling along.

Sue: Has my position this year as Certification Teacher made a difference?

Cindy: Your coming out of the classroom has garnered a lot of respect. People know that you know what you are talking about. Now, if questioned, they might recognize your role in starting the change process.

Sue: I'm really not concerned about having my role recognized. I'm very aware that all I did was start something in motion. What has happened here reflects the work and commitment of everyone.

WHAT IS THE IMPACT OF ASSUMING LEADERSHIP ROLES ON THE CLASSROOM?

The profound personal changes which result from leadership experiences have an effect in the classroom.

Cindy: My leadership roles have affected the way I teach. As I took on new roles and felt successful, I gained the confidence to make changes in the way I structure my classroom. I think other

146

teachers here felt the same way. Because we were no longer just voiceless faces in faculty meetings, we knew we had the power to make the changes in our classrooms that we knew we should.

Five years ago I saw myself as a pretty good teacher, with a lot to offer kids. I worked hard and wanted to do the best possible job, but I was a real traditional teacher. I stayed within the realm of my textbooks. When new programs were brought in, I did my best. When I tried to question some programs, I was told, "We've already spent the money." I recognized that I had strengths and weaknesses, but I didn't feel I had a way to make improvements except by taking graduate courses. Right after I completed my Master's, I had a baby and didn't have the time for courses. Besides, my Master's didn't really help me with what I felt was my greatest weakness—working with remedial or low achievement students. Although I took courses in my under-graduate program on working with those kids, theory into practice didn't always work.

Sue: I was hired to teach language arts, which is a separate subject, divorced from reading and literature. Since there was no written curriculum at the time, I had to figure out what I was going to teach. In the past, teachers taught grammar and mechanics, using Warriner's as their text. I knew that I didn't want to do that; I wanted to teach kids to write, and to get them involved in learning. At first, I thought I could do that simply by motivating them with exciting assignments. I discovered quickly that didn't work for all students. Although I liked to write and had done well on compositions in school, I didn't understand how writers work, or how to teach writing. For the first few years, I floundered around, trying to find a focus for my curriculum that would be meaningful and engaging.

After several years, I stumbled onto process writing and attended some workshops. I changed my approach, and it was a big improvement. I was involved in the development of a K–8 language arts curriculum based on the writing process. Over the next five years, I saw an enormous improvement in the level of writing skills in my students, who were getting years of consistent writing instruction. That was a good lesson for me, because I saw that the results of a change may take years to be fully evident. My class was still very structured, however. I developed topics that allowed kids to draw on their own experiences to personalize their writing, and I offered choices, but they were still my topics. I was in charge of my classroom; that was very important to me.

I always saw teaching as experimentation and was never satisfied with what I was doing. I didn't really know where to get help for improvement. I had a friend in another school district who was an excellent teacher. I observed him once, and he helped me get started, but it was hard to maintain that contact, and I was basically on my own. I didn't feel I could admit that I didn't have it all together. There was no administrative supervision at all; I wasn't observed by anyone for the first four or five years. When I finally was, I was nervous, but I also knew I had things under control, and would be at least OK. By that time, I was a veteran.

As part of our training in peer coaching, we had to teach model lessons in small groups. I was really nervous when it was my turn. Standing up in front of my peers and allowing them to watch me teach was frightening. I had no idea whether they would think I was a good teacher. Maybe I was really a fraud. It turned out to be a positive, supportive experience. After several demonstration lessons, I got to the point where I could say to the group, "I really don't know how to do this next part. I need some help." That experience was a real turning point. It was OK to ask for help, to not be the expert, to not always have it all together. After this, I worked closely with a group of other teachers. We were frequently in each other's rooms. I began to seek out ways to team with colleagues. I felt like my teaching began to really improve during this time.

I see my development as a teacher as a continuum. I can't really think of any dramatic turning points in my beliefs about teaching and learning, but I certainly know a great deal more than I did a few years ago. I know I still have a lot to learn.

Cindy: For me, there was a turning point. Before I read the research on heterogeneous and homogeneous grouping, I felt comfortable with the way I taught. I felt kids were getting what they needed, and were being successful. I was an original member of the Grouping Committee, but had to resign because of home pressures. Initially, I was scared and resistant to the research we read about grouping. I was getting information about what was best for kids, but also looking at what was best for me, knowing that the teacher needs to feel comfortable. That year was full of self-doubt. Was I a good teacher? Despite what my evaluations said, I didn't feel like I was. What I was doing didn't seem to jell with what *research says* about what is best for kids, and how they learn. No matter what had happened in the rest of my life, there was that one constant: I was a good teacher. Then *research says* that perhaps I wasn't. When I doubted that, it was awful. It blew me away emotionally. That's why I made a drastic change, jumped in with both feet. Knowing students have varying abilities, I immediately restructured my classes into cooperative learning groups in order to give them expertise in working together and listening to each other. In the past, I had tended to stay with what was safe. But when what's safe is giving you problems, that's hard.

Sue: How do you see your role as a teacher now?

Cindy: I see myself more as a facilitator for kids to learn. I feel confident I have enough skills and knowledge to understand what my kids need. I know they can learn, one way or another. To me, a good teacher is knowledgeable in content area and methods and is fair and consistent with students. I think I am. A good teacher is flexible and adaptive. If something didn't work one way, it can be changed. What I'm afraid of is that I don't want to be looked at as someone who experiments with every new thing, someone who takes flyers all the time. I want people to realize that when I change, I'm grounded in knowing why I'm doing it. I have good reasons for making the changes that I make.

For example, next year I don't plan to issue textbooks. That's a really big change for me. The reasoning behind it is this: I'll have heterogeneous groups. The texts I have just won't be suitable for all kids in my classes. I don't want to deal with three or four texts and different groups within my classes. Instead, I'll have thematic units. I know what I want kids to get out of each unit. The objectives will be the same for all kids, but how they meet them may differ.

When things bomb in my class, I feel I can go to other teachers or administrators for ideas, or just to cry on someone's shoulder. I usually go inside myself. Sometimes I turn to journals. I may go to Marylyn [MIL consultant] or to Michele or Debbie [teachers]. I also talk about problems with my team. I have more time now; common planning time is really helpful. I don't have the sense of isolation I used to have.

Sue: Is it a change in the circumstances or in your own attitude?

Cindy: It's probably a combination of both. There is now a level of comfort in this building where you can go to someone and say, "That bombed." I couldn't do that before. I knew people felt I was a good teacher. It wasn't that I wanted to maintain a facade, but people didn't take me seriously when I said I needed help, because I was a *good* teacher. Maybe it was my own insecurity, so I projected this *good teacher* image to others so that I didn't have to admit I didn't always know what I was doing. Now, I'd tell the whole world I don't always know. Now, if I want to try something new, I'll jump right in. This is a radical change from the person who, if she needed exactly 25 copies of a worksheet, would make 40, "just in case." People can't believe it—I can't believe it. And I feel better about the teacher I am now than the teacher I was a few years ago.

Teaching is perceived as a job with a lot of control in the classroom. To give that up, when trying something new like cooperative learning, is really hard. As teachers we have to learn to let go, to step back. We tend to think that no one else can teach our subject as well as we can; we want to *fix* others. We

150

need to let students find their own way; it may not be our way, but it's just as effective.

Sue: That's a tough lesson to learn. Last year, I made a major change in my class. I switched to a writing lab approach. The summer before, I read Nancie Atwell's book and decided to give it a try. I let go of all my structured assignments and prepared to let kids select their own topics. I made checklists and prepared everything I'd need before school started. I realized that I was giving up much of my control as a teacher; maybe I thought that I could retain a little control by being super-organized. I even fell into the trap of thinking I could take Atwell's model and impose it in my classroom. Of course I couldn't; I had to modify and adapt.

I was generally pleased with the way it worked. With some exceptions, kids took responsibility for their writing. I liked having the time for lots of individual writing conferences. I sometimes was frustrated by the informal talking that went on when I was conferencing; I knew they were socializing, not discussing their writing. I remember saying to one class in late March, "It makes me uncomfortable when this much talking is going on; I'm afraid it's keeping you from getting your work done." They told me they were working, but they also needed to be able to socialize a bit. In effect, they were asking for me to trust their understanding of their own needs. I thought about the amount and quality of the writing they'd done that year, and mentally compared it with the years when I'd been in charge of the topics. They were right; they'd done at least as well and probably better. I was able to let them take responsibility for deciding when and how to write. However, I was less successful in giving up my need to tell them how to improve their writing. I tried using questions to help them figure out what needed improvement. All too often, when that didn't work, I told them. I realize that I was sacrificing the development of their thinking to get them to my goal. I wasn't always able to act as a facilitator for their learning, because of my image of the teacher as being "in control." I still have a lot to learn about teaching.

Cindy: The administrators we've had here the last few years made it easy for teachers to change if we wanted to. They provided support and encouragement. There was a real easy relationship between administration and teachers. It made me less fearful of making mistakes. If something went wrong, it wasn't the end of the world. They helped us keep change in perspective. The entire atmosphere that's been fostered here—that it's OK to take risks—has made a tremendous difference for me. I feel more creative, and I have more fun. And I know I'm a better teacher now than I was back then. I remember when Tom Parker, our former assistant principal, gave as one of his reasons for leaving Wells to accept a principalship elsewhere something like, "How can I tell kids to make the most of opportunities, to take a chance, to challenge themselves, if I don't dare to myself?" That sums it up for me, too, and expresses how I approach my teaching and my team leader role now.

CONCLUSION

Several common themes emerge from our stories; one is *isolation versus connection.* Both of us remember our earlier isolation in contrast to the way we work now. In spite of teaching the same grade and closely related subject, Cindy and I didn't collaborate—or even discuss what happened in our classrooms. I remember the lack of support I had for learning about teaching early in my career, when I was isolated in my classroom. This memory led to my later interest in developing a peer support system for new teachers. My leadership experiences helped break my isolation. My decision to apply for the Mastery In Learning Project was motivated by a sense that something was still missing, that isolation continued for the majority of teachers in the school who were not involved in the peer support process as new teachers or as mentors.

Lieberman and Miller (1978) describe closed interactions as the norm in most schools; teachers prefer to keep distance rather than talk about teaching in order to preserve their classroom autonomy. They limit their interchanges to jousting or griping, because "it pays to be separate. We learn that in our isolation we have strength" (1978, p. 61). Those norms certainly existed at Wells Junior High five years ago. Cindy mentions the "bitching and griping" that went on as something that was accepted by everyone. Now she recognizes the value of connections with colleagues that include talking openly about teaching, especially being able to share difficulties and problems. She regularly turns to several individuals, both teachers and administrators, to talk about teaching. She also discusses problems with her team. She no longer has the sense of isolation she used to have. Both of us see close connections with our peers as a major source of strength.

A second theme is the shift to seeing ourselves as *facilitators of student learning rather than givers of information.* For Cindy, the change was abrupt, a result of thinking about the research she was reading and comparing it to her own classroom experiences, while for me it was more gradual. Both of us recognize the sense of loss of control which accompanies the shift. Cindy acknowledges the need to step back and let students find their own way at the same time she experiences the discomfort of letting go. It was difficult for me to let go of my need to have students reach my goals for their writing and let them establish their own goals. Control is a key issue for teachers. Because of our need to gain the participation of large numbers of youngsters in tasks we set for them, we place a premium on activities which involve as little noise and confusion as possible. When we are in charge in the front of the room, we know we have things under our control. We know our peers and supervisors in the past have judged us by our control of the classroom.

Letting go of that control in order to help students learn more effectively makes us vulnerable to mistakes and criticism.

When we become *learners* with our students instead of experts who know all the answers, we take a significant personal risk. I remember vividly my first experiences with teaching demonstration lessons in a peer coaching class, my fears that colleagues would discover I was a fraud. Cindy talks about projecting the facade of "the good teacher" rather than admitting that sometimes she wasn't sure what she was doing. For both of us, being able to put aside that facade, ask for help, take risks and make mistakes openly was a difficult step. However, the consequences are positive, for our students and ourselves. The teacher who takes few risks, who is always carefully prepared, sends a message to students that risk-taking is not permissible. Cindy remembers a former principal saying that he can't expect students to take risks, to accept challenges, if he himself is unwilling to do so. Students "need models of thinking as a human, imperfect and attainable activity" (Belenky, Clinchy, Goldberger, and Tarule 1986, p. 217). As we think publicly about our subjects and our teaching, we model learning for our students.

Two images for our new roles as teacher-leaders also emerge from this conversation. The first is the metaphor of *voice*. Cindy talks about the importance to her of gaining and keeping a voice. In a school where teachers are leaders, we are all encouraged to express our opinions and to take others' into account in a mutual search for our truth. We encourage the expression of diverse ideas and beliefs, allowing for the tentative nature of evolving thought. For me, encouraging others to develop their own voices has sometimes required me to still my own.

The second is *leaving*. As we have developed as leaders in our own unique ways, we have left old, comfortable habits and ways of being. We have left the comfort of silence or of voice. We have left behind control, being in charge, knowing all the answers. We have left being able to blame others when things go wrong. We have left our role as the visible leader or the quiet watcher. In our leaving has been our growth. *Growth* is ultimately the common thread in our different stories.

REFERENCES

Belenky, M.; Clinchy, B.; Goldberger, N.; and Tarule, J. 1986. *Women's ways of knowing.* New York: Basic Books.

Lieberman, A., and Miller, L. 1978. The social realities of teaching. *Teachers College Record* 80:54–68.

Lieberman, A., and Miller, L. 1986. School improvement: Themes and variations. *Teachers College Record* 86:4–16.

McDonald, J. P. 1986. Raising the teacher's voice and the ironic role of theory. *Harvard Educational Review* 56:355–78.

Part Two:
REFLECTIONS

Chapter 6

TEACHER LEADERSHIP: WHAT ARE WE LEARNING?

by Ann Lieberman

Teacher participation in leadership is critical to the process of school change. Conditions necessary for teacher leadership include a vision and set of values, structures and contexts, and time. Teacher leadership roles are expanding; formal roles institutionalize new ways of working, and informal and emergent ones help to build collaborative cultures. Teacher leadership requires skills and abilities. Teacher learning and a continuous process of evaluation are at the core of the new professionalism. We need to continue our efforts to understand and build collaborative cultures for learner-centered schools.

As the move to restructure schools continues, it is becoming increasingly evident that teacher participation in leadership may be the most critical component of the entire process of change. What we are beginning to see is that teacher involvement in their own learning has powerful effects on students, on the culture of the school and on teachers' own sense of efficacy. We need to continue to learn from experience, from reflection, as well as from lessons already learned. What follows are some reflections on where we have been, what we are learning in this ongoing process, and future implications for teacher leadership in the building of a collaborative culture in schools that are learner-centered.

EARLY LESSONS

Only a few years ago the notion of teacher leadership in

159

both research and practice circles was a new idea—new in the sense that there were no prescribed descriptions of what a "teacher leader" was supposed to do, and new because leadership, up until that time, was only meant for those in the principal's role. Early studies were concerned with questions about the concept itself: What is teacher leadership anyway? How do teachers feel about leading? What will their colleagues say when one steps out of the classroom to expand the teacher role? How will such people be selected? And by whose criteria? (Diercks, et al. 1988). One had the sense that a new idea had burst upon the scene and that there was nervousness all around. Principals were nervous because it seemed like an encroachment on their territory. Teachers were nervous because their peers were suspect of some people trying to find yet another way to leave the classroom; and those in positions of teacher leadership were nervous because they were charting new territory—often with little or no preparation—in a culture unused to teachers being out of the classroom (unless it was for a field trip).

Today the move to restructure schools to make them more learner-centered is being coupled with the powerful move to professionalize teaching. The dual goals then—to rethink how schools are organized to deal with the student as the center, while changing the way teachers participate is nothing short of revolutionary. We are not talking about a simple new intervention, but rather the changing of a whole culture.

LEADING: SOME NECESSARY CONDITIONS

It is becoming very clear that teacher leadership roles must be a part of an overall *vision* and a *set of values* that *accepts* and *expects* teachers to participate in leadership. In places where a new role is introduced, unrelated to a larger vision of greater teacher participation, teachers will not be able to sustain the systemic challenges inherent in a change of such magnitude. Where there is a broad vision for a school, such as creating "A School as a Center for Inquiry," teachers are encouraged to see the school as larger than their own classroom, change as a legitimate process for everyone, and leadership as an important part of making such changes. Although those who take on these new roles will have to work out their feelings of uneasiness in working with their peers, legitimating these roles is critical if they are to take root and grow.

Teacher leaders need to have a *structure for their work*. But that structure is not universal and indeed appears to vary in different schools and contexts. For some, it is a school site committee where teachers are encouraged to take leadership. For others it is a restructuring project that starts with a curriculum area, or several teachers who decide to do whole language, or a teacher who becomes the coordinator for a new interdisciplinary team, or a formal teacher leadership role created at the district level. Whatever the new structure for work, faculty see that it legitimates doing things differently and come to accept the fact that teachers who are well-respected, get along with their peers and are knowledgeable, can provide leadership for the school in a variety of capacities. Such a structure must enable teachers to experiment, to talk about what they are learning, and to re-arrange resources to support student learning. Those contexts that support change at every level (school, district, state) provide strong messages to teachers and principals that positive changes are to be taken seriously, and that this is not yet another "innovation" that will be gone come September.

Making decisions about what teacher leaders are to do and when they are to do it inevitably leads to problems of *time:* time to learn; time to talk with one another; time to get new materials (or make them); time to experiment, reflect, talk about it; time to create; time to deal with the inevitable conflict that comes with a clash of values; time to build collegial relationships where there have been none. Time becomes the most valuable resource of all—whether borrowed or stolen, spent wisely or foolishly, or restructured as it inevitably must be.

Teacher leadership roles are proliferating in greater *variety* than many thought possible. Formal roles are the easiest to create, but informal and emergent ones may be far more powerful in changing the way teachers lead. The former is important because it institutionalizes a new role for teachers and, over time, people come to expect teachers to lead. When real financial outlays of money are forthcoming, the role is seen as part of the fabric of a school. But informal roles, and those that emerge as schools participate in major restructuring efforts, have the power to change the culture of the school since they become integral to the changes taking place that beget new needs for knowledge and support. Teachers, with their variety of talents and interests, are becoming researchers, scholars, coordinators, curriculum developers, process consultants, content experts, and much more.

Teachers assuming such roles help to breed a continuous *process of evaluation:* not the evaluation that makes judgments that offer little help for improvement, but evaluation that consistently and constantly asks searching questions, creates new means to get at tough problems, new ways to approach learning for students and adults, and always seeks to find out how things can be done better. This kind of evaluation makes assumptions about teachers as leaders as well as learners and is at the core what is meant by professionalism.

TEACHER LEARNING

The learning that is going on among teachers is powerful. We are literally creating a new language and a new way of thinking about teaching and student learning. Giving students more responsibility and encouraging them to work collaboratively; connecting reading, writing, and speaking; doing action research in our own classrooms; inventing more integrated ways of thinking about student engagement—all provide the basis for examining the role of the teacher- and student-learner. By engaging in a greater variety of roles that get at student learning, the *gap between theory and practice* becomes more

162

evident. Teachers and heretofore distant researchers become a team bringing different perspectives to similar questions (e.g., investigating how *gender issues* intertwine with issues of bureaucracy). Collaboration and recognizing leadership in a variety of forms is acceptable only if one accepts leadership as *a set of functions*—rather than an assigned formal role—*that can be accomplished by a variety of people.*

By studying teacher leaders we are finding out that there are *skills and abilities* that help make a more effective leader and that many of them can be labeled and learned (Lieberman, Saxl, and Miles 1988). We are also finding out that the process of change can be studied, understood and used as a tool to aid in restructuring a school. (For example, if we know that new roles and new structures create uneasiness and often resistance, then we will not be surprised when it happens, or feel that it is impossible for things to really change.) We see that bringing a staff together to discuss restructuring schools to make them learner-centered will produce *conflict.* Learning how to make such conflict productive and work through the problems inherent in the clashes of values over teaching styles, approaches to students, curriculum, and the many personal and organizational slights that are a part of school life, is a major challenge.

In the process of learning how to mount these new roles, we are creating a new language for work along with some new expectations for the professionalization of teaching. It is a language that includes terms such as *collaboration, problem solving, problem posing, creating new knowledge, using research knowledge, doing teacher research, peer evaluation, authentic assessment,* etc. It is also a language of hope, of participation, and of connection with one another. This language symbolizes both a new set of ideas and the real change taking place in the way schools go about working with students, as the ideas and the reality interact to change the way we work in schools in a fundamental way.

163

BUILDING A COLLABORATIVE CULTURE

In the process of restructuring the learning environment for students, teachers are, *perhaps for the first time,* being given recognition for the expertise they have with students. But more than that, when teachers' abilities are acknowledged, they find it easier to acknowledge student possibilities. This dramatic shift—legitimating teacher expertise on the one hand and student-centered learning on the other—becomes the fulcrum for the development of teacher leadership and for changing a school from an isolated set of individuals to a collaborative culture. Instead of being a member of the bureaucratic chain taking orders from someone else, teachers become empowered and therefore responsible for making critical decisions about students, learning, participation, the community, and evaluation and accountability.

Professionalizing teaching to better serve students will only come if we gain the knowledge that enables us to continue to grow and learn. How will such knowledge be made available to teachers—both the old and the new knowledge being created as a part of the restructuring process? How can we make room to learn while the school is changing? What structures will enable teachers to try out new ideas with students and be supported in the process? How can we continue to codify the variety of teacher leadership roles without making them so formalistic that they lose their relevance and importance? How can we restructure time in schools so that students are better served and teachers have time to facilitate for their learning?

We know what a bureaucracy looks like and how it works. Although we rail against it, it is comfortable and familiar. But we do not yet know what a collaborative culture looks like or how to build one. Teachers who take leadership roles in schools struggling to do this will help us see the limits and possibilities. Researchers will help us conceptualize these new roles in partnership with teachers. We have a long way to go, but building a new paradigm for leadership has a healthy start.

164

REFERENCES

Diercks, K., et al. 1988. *Teacher leadership: Commitment and challenge.* Seattle: Puget Sound Educational Consortium.

Lieberman, A.; Saxl, E. R.; and Miles, M. B. 1988. Teacher leadership: Ideology and practice. In *Building a professional culture in schools,* ed. A. Lieberman, 148–66. New York: Teachers College Press.

Chapter 7

A VISION OF TEACHER LEADERSHIP

by Eliot Wigginton

The issues of teacher leadership are complex. Teacher leaders who are leaders of teachers must be credible to their peers. The author envisions a new style of leadership of teachers, by their peers, which grows out of a common vision of what they want their schools to be, with flexible time to allow teachers to reconnect their rich body of practical knowledge with the ideas of classic educational scholars. Preferring the term scout *to* leader, *he reminds us to include students in our quest for shared leadership.*

One thing these essays reveal is that the issue of teacher leadership is devilishly complicated. And it doesn't help matters that the phrase itself is frustratingly ambiguous: Does it mean acts of leadership by teachers, or the leading of teachers?

Clearly, the essays in this book would have us focus on the latter, which forces the question, leadership by whom? By an outside authority like Madeline Hunter or one of her clones? By a member of the administration or the central office staff? By a peer—or a former peer?

At this point the issue divides, it seems to me, into two categories: *outside leadership* versus *inside leadership.* Leadership by anyone who does not work full time in the same building of those to be led, I'd label outside leadership. I'd even call the curriculum director in our tiny county an outside leader. Despite the fact that she was recently "one of us"—a social studies teacher in our public high school—she now works in a different building, we see her only infrequently, and so she comes to us, when she comes, from "outside."

Some people persist in calling me a teacher leader. If that is true, then whenever I am working with other teachers away from the public school where I am employed, I'm an outsider. None of this discussion is to imply negative connotations for that distinction, by the way. It's merely to make the point that people in that category face distinct dilemmas that can threaten their effectiveness as leaders—questions of credibility, motive, and invitation. Sara, in Ann Kilcher's essay, would resonate to that.

And teachers who would be led seem to want those questions dealt with up front. They are at the heart of the inquiries I get over and over again from any audience of teachers whenever I am speaking at a conference or an inservice meeting, or conducting a workshop or a graduate level course. It reminds me of the experience I had in the summer of 1965 in San Antonio, Texas. In some crazy, romantic, youthful burst of exuberance, I had taken a summer off from college to work my way across this country to California and back, alone, camping out and surviving on the money I earned doing odd jobs in strange places. In Texas, I found a two-week situation selling ads by phone for a newspaper called *The Jewish Press*, the slogan of which was, "Serving Judaism in the Southwest." I was given a stack of index cards, each bearing the name of a business, its owner, and his or her phone number. On my first call, after I had finished my sales pitch, the owner asked, "What year is it?"

"1965," I replied, at which point the owner hung up.

I went into the office of the Catholic who ran the paper, told him what had happened, and, after he finished laughing, was told that if I answered, "2062" (or something like that), I'd have better luck.

Next call, same question. "2062."

"Year of the what?" the question came.

"Oh," said my boss when I confronted him with this new obstacle. "It's the year of the ox. Sorry. Forgot to tell you."

And so on, through a roll call of questions designed to get at my credibility, exactly like the teachers who, before we can *really* talk, ask, "How many classes a day did you say you teach?"

and, "How big are your classes?" and, "Gifted and talented, or mixed ability?"

Inside leadership, by contrast, I'd call leadership by folks who are in the building full-time—administrators, department heads, full time teachers—and who consequently are, or should be, more sensitive than outsiders to the school's unique culture. It's in this category that I'd place the kind of leader the authors of these essays are most fascinated by: the leader of teachers who is, himself or herself, one of them. Leadership of teachers by their own peers, as these essays clearly reveal, has its own distinct dilemmas, all of which must also be confronted. Who chooses? To whom does she report? What's her relationship to the principal going to be? What kinds of tasks should she take on: administrative, visionary, pedagogical? Who says? Is she going to be paid extra? Will she still teach a full load? What's she going to try to get us to do? Where's the time going to come from? What if we vote to do something and the principal vetoes it? What about the teachers who don't want to be led, thank you? Who *wants* any of this noise anyway?

Questions like these are tough for me to respond to with any authority because, in the twenty-five years I have been teaching, I have never been part of a faculty where there was anything resembling a teacher leader (except the old paradigm of the department head who files our lesson plans somewhere every Monday, and that's not what we're talking about here). I've never seen it happen first hand. I've only read about it in books like this. And I suspect, by the way, that my experience is not unique. I'll bet the reason for it not happening in our school is not unique, either: There simply has never been an invitation. If the idea of any of this has ever flickered like a tiny light in the minds of any of the six principals for whom I've worked, they never shared that fact with any of us.

Intellectually, though, I can see compelling reasons for extending the invitation and dealing with the dilemmas that arise. In our school, for example, there are pockets of expertise—the teacher who uses small group instruction effec-

169

tively in her classroom; another who is taking a graduate course that has taught her how to do classroom-based research; another who, on his own, has looked into Nancie Atwell's work—but that expertise is never formally acknowledged as a valuable resource, and consequently it is never spread among us, and most are oblivious to its existence. Thus, we cannot see ourselves as a collection of fairly remarkable people who represent strengths and solutions to all our problems. We see only our individual, personal burdens, and we carry those solitary weights like anvils.

There are also teachers on our faculty who genuinely care about our purpose, and whose enthusiasm could lift our spirits and give us a sense of momentum, but they might as well be enthusiastic about asphalt, for all the good their concern is allowed to do the rest of us. Having never been led by anyone to come together and forge a shared vision of the school we want to be part of, we have no sense of mission or purpose other than that which we can generate within our own individual hearts, with a few colleagues, and with our kids. The potential leaders among us, if allowed to do so, could help change all that.

Here's another reason: The universe of teaching is filled with magnificent, clarifying insights about learning, about children, about our craft. I uncovered some of these six years ago when, on a scavenger hunt for advice I could use in my classroom, I went back and reread some of the philosophy I must have read in college but had long since forgotten—Dewey, Maslow, Piaget. A couple of pages into Chapter One of *Experience and Education,* where Dewey outlines the distinctions between traditional and progressive styles and warns us about the pitfalls inherent in both, and I was shaking my head in amazement. For nearly twenty years, I had been struggling with both styles of instruction, ricocheting back and forth between them, floundering around with only the vaguest notions of why I was using either ("Well, this activity seems to work pretty well the last time I tried it; maybe I'll do it again this year"), and suddenly I was handed perspective. It was as if I were up in the air above myself, looking down and watching myself struggle, and now I understood. Since I have begun teaching summer graduate courses for teachers, I have discovered that most of those folks are in the same situation I was: In our education courses, we were exposed to philosophers like John Dewey—at least we think we *must* have been, somehow—but because we had no experience base to relate the insights to, we left them all behind. And there's the point: Now that we are practitioners, we can respond instantly to the wisdom of those who gave their professional lives to the study of education. The problem is that few of us have the time or energy on our own to go back and review all that work. (I had to take a sabbatical to do that reading I was able to do.) Another role for teacher leaders, in other words, can be to divide up carefully selected materials among themselves and search for those ideas that could be constructive for us all—philosophy processed and shared by people we have come to trust. Likewise the recommendations of various state and national commissions (I'd be willing to bet that very few members of our faculty read *A Nation At Risk*) as well as the design of, and progress being made by, the various reform initiatives.

Of course, the most persuasive reason of all for encouraging and nourishing the potential leaders among us, as these essays show convincingly, is the impact such efforts have on our personal and professional growth. That translates into immediate benefits for the kids we all care so much about.

Let me stay with this notion for the moment of a new style of leadership of teachers, from inside, by their peers. Given the dilemmas involved, one of the contributions the essays in this book make is, out of the heat off battle, to move the conversation forward. That's especially true with Lynne Miller's narrative about the Narragansett School. One effect of reading that is, now that I see the whole notion is *possible,* all sorts of variations on the theme begin to swim around in my brain. Suddenly I see myself teaching in a school where several peers, chosen by us, have led us to the point where we have a vision for the school we want, a list of the characteristics and principles by which it will operate day-to-day, and a list of the things we now have to have or know in order to get where we want to be. We know these lists will be changed constantly as we uncover new ideas, but there's enough there that we have been able to begin. We have divided ourselves up into teams of scouts to go find or generate the information we need. We are working toward having an in-house Dewey expert, a Piaget expert, a collaborative learning expert, a writing process expert, a classroom research expert, an assessment expert. Each of them will collect what we already know among ourselves, and add to that knowledge base. We have generated a list of names of faculty members we know and respect at nearby colleges of education, and several of us have recruited them to give us a hand. One of us has decided that former students, both dropouts and college graduates, might have insights into our school and into education that we could use, and so she and the students in one of her current sociology classes have designed a project through which they will interview those graduates and compile the results. Her kids have already advanced the notion that it might be beneficial to get a group of those dropouts together, bring them to a faculty meeting, and enlist their help in designing a dropout prevention program for our current ninth graders. A math teacher and her students have taken our current school budget, and faculty-generated grocery list of needs, and next week, a group of those students, as part of the research they've been doing, will make a presentation to us about some equipment purchase options and possible sources of funds. Another teacher and one of his classes are working with the janitors every day during fifth period to figure out ways to implement a recycling program on campus.

And we know that if we think of ourselves not as *leaders* (since none of us is comfortable with that distinction) but as *scouts,* going out with our kids to find useful information, process it, and bring it home, that true, home-grown, natural leadership will emerge in unlikely places among both faculty and students, and we will seize on that, and acknowledge and celebrate it as it appears, and participate with those people in redesigning their roles in our school in appropriate ways.

And my role? Let's see. What piece of all this do I want?

Actually, maybe the best use of my time is to stop dreaming crazy dreams and see if I can figure out a way to get the principal of the Rabun County High School to just extend an invitation. First things first.

What a long journey this has suddenly become.

THE CONTRIBUTORS

Robert M. McClure is Director of the Mastery In Learning Consortium within the NEA National Center for Innovation. He formerly directed the NEA Mastery In Learning Project and served as Associate Director of NEA's Instruction and Professional Development unit. Long an advocate for curriculum reform and returning to faculty their rightful roles as key decision makers in schools, McClure has helped develop many of the Association's programs and publications on school improvement.

Carol Livingston is Assistant Professor of Education at Catholic University of America, consultant with the NEA National Center for Innovation, and former Coordinator for Research in the NEA Mastery In Learning Project. She has spent 15 years in public education as a classroom teacher and teacher specialist. Her professional interests include teacher education with particular emphasis on teacher reflection, teacher involvement in school reform, and teachers as researchers. She is co-editor (with Shari Castle) of *Teachers and Research in Action* (NEA, 1989).

Patricia A. Wasley is Senior Researcher for School Change for the Coalition of Essential Schools, Brown University, where her role is to document the benefits and barriers to change for teachers, administrators, students, and parents. She recently coordinated a teacher leadership project for the National Network for Educational Renewal. She has taught high school, worked in a regional educational agency, and consulted with school districts in their work of restructuring. She is the author of *Teacher Leadership: Problems, Paradoxes and Possibilities* (Teachers College Press, 1991).

Carolyn Fay is Director of the Leadership Institute for the Future of Teaching (LIFT), an organization dedicated to leadership development for teachers who want to combine the roles of teaching and leading. She formerly directed the Indianapolis Public Schools Office of Professional Development and Teacher Center, which she founded in 1978, after fifteen years as a classroom teacher of English.

Ann Kilcher is an educational consultant with the Paideia Consulting Group in Halifax, Nova Scotia. She has worked actively with teachers and administrators for the past decade, assisting them to improve teaching and schools. Her most recent work has focused on team building and collaborative relationships in schools. She is co-author (with Nancy Watson) of *Peer Coaching* (Ontario Secondary School Teachers' Federation, 1990).

Lynne Miller is Professor of Education at the University of Southern Maine, where she directs the Southern Maine Partnership and the university's teacher education program. She has been a public school teacher and administrator and has written widely in the areas of staff development, school improvement, and restructuring. She is co-author (with Ann Lieberman) of *Teachers, Their World and Their Work* (ASCD, 1984) and *Staff Development for the Nineties* (Teachers College Press, 1991).

Susan Walters is Certification Teacher for the Wells-Ogunquit School District in southern Maine, where she coordinates a peer support system for new teachers and provides supervision for teacher interns through the district's professional development partnership with the University of Southern Maine. She served as chair of the Mastery In Learning Steering Committee at Wells Junior High for four years and has authored several publications about the Project.

Ann Lieberman is Professor of Curriculum and Teaching and Co-Director of the National Center for Restructuring Education, Schools and Teaching at Teachers College, Columbia University, and President of the American Educational Research Association. Her interests are in teaching, teacher leadership, restructuring, and collaborative ways of working with universities, schools, and teachers. She has written numerous books on teaching, staff development, and teacher leadership.

Eliot Wigginton is a high school teacher in Rabun County, Georgia, and director of the Foxfire Fund, Inc., a nonprofit educational corporation he founded in 1968. Widely recognized as an author and spokesperson for experiential education, he has conducted workshops for teachers and consulted with public schools nation-wide. He and his English students continue to produce *Foxfire Magazine.* He has served on numerous boards and advisory councils, and his work has been the focus of books, theater, and television.